THE PAINTER

Ewen MacDonald

HEDDON PUBLISHING

First edition published in 2017 by Heddon Publishing.

ISBN 978-0-9934870-8-8

Cover design by Catherine Clarke

Book design and layout by Katharine Smith,
Heddon Publishing.

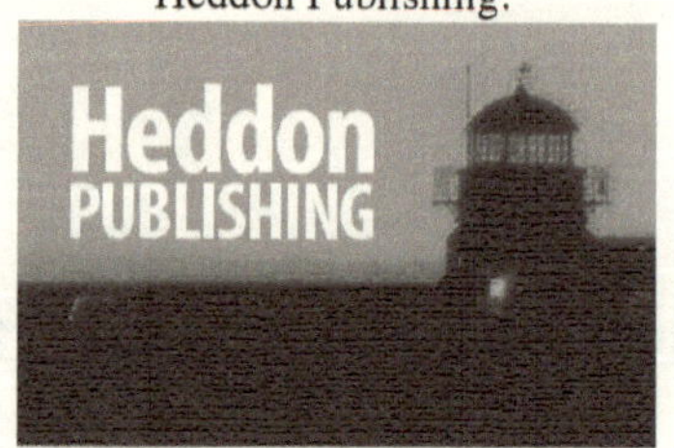

www.heddonpublishing.com
www.facebook.com/heddonpublishing
@PublishHeddon

For Carol
For Everything

Born and raised in the Scottish Highlands, Ewen MacDonald has also been a resident of Inverness, the Isle of Skye, the Channel Islands and Leicester. He has a degree in history and has also studied film, photography and architecture.

Throughout his career, he has variously been an electrician, civil servant, trade unionist, general factotum, plongeur, and, for a brief spell, a gallerist. He currently works as a freelance writer and photographer. He is married with one son and lives in Cornwall.

CHAPTER 1

He knew something was wrong when the chair began talking to him. A gaping hole had developed along the right side of the seat. He watched, intrigued, as its reflection in the mirror spluttered and stammered into a slurred dialogue. The words were contorted in a spasmic gurgitation, 'I have willed into being. I am in mirror. I reflect that which I am incapable of witnessing.'

The only thing he could say with any certainty was that this phenomenon had never occurred before in his life.

Transfixed, he drew himself over to the chair. The right side bore no sign of damage. He inspected every inch with wary fingers before turning once more towards the mirror. The reflection revealed a dark, brooding abyss cut into the striped, multi-coloured seat, and appeared sadly desolate. He pushed his left hand cautiously into the mirror, which warped inwardly towards the dark void in the chair. He could feel nothing. There was a curious lack of substance, as though the façade of events had taken on an edgeless existence.

The mirror rusted and dissolved before him, the smashed pieces falling from around his hand. The chair's upholstery appeared to melt and ooze its way onto the floor. He began to retch violently. His surroundings became diluted and he was left alone on the floor, gripping hold of his haemorrhaging wrist.

Opening his eyes some time later, the room came into focus with a rare intensity. His right palm was lodged beneath his face. The colour red filled his vision; it was in his eyes, his hair, his clothes, and it had glued his hand to his face. He levered himself gently from the ground. His hand and face detached from each other with a slight tearing sound. There was dried blood everywhere. In the corner of the room stood an empty bottle of wine and in the middle of the floor a smashed crystal glass. The palm of his left hand was deeply gashed. The blood, which had momentarily congealed, began to well up again as he stretched his hand and the blood dripped onto the dark parquet flooring. He squeezed his fingers together in a sponge-like motion, as though wringing his mortality from his flesh. His black suit was stained with blood and vomit and his shirt buttons, which had been torn off, lay floating in the scarlet-and-mustard coloured viscera.

He stumbled his way towards the large belle époque mirror which had caused his injury, but it had disappeared from sight. To be sure, he felt along the smooth, empty concrete wall with his uninjured hand; but the mirror had disappeared, along with the chair. Instead, there was an inch-deep gash in the wall, which he explored with his fingers along its one-metre length. The texture inside was hard and grainy, not at all what he had expected. He picked at a few grains of the porous substance until he chipped the nail of his index finger clean off. He let out a deep, primal howl at the pain before sucking at the finger greedily. The metallic taste ran along his tongue and down his throat. He choked and gagged before spitting a mouthful onto the wall. The deep red flecks sparkled translucently against the expanse of bright greyness of the empty wall. He unzipped himself and urinated over the unblemished flooring.

His piss stank of fresh spring vegetables, strong spirits, and semen. He knelt down and sniffed disgustedly at the vulgar puddle, then tentatively licked a few drops of the pungent broth. He could taste nothing; he was dead.

There was no corpse to be found in the room. Only a crumpled grey duvet and matching single pillow on the floor. He scanned the space for his body. He lifted the sheets and found a pair of soiled underpants. It was the only evidence of a life once existed. He wondered if there had been a woman anywhere. He checked for the residue of female habitation. Then he sought out an example of masturbation. He could find neither.

His injured hand began to ache. It was the discovery of something. Pain had its answers: he was not deceased. A source of light on one wall drew his attention. He moved cautiously towards it and pulled up a white blind. Outside, a stone patio led to a rectangular pool filled with still, green water. On the patio sat a lone wooden sun-lounger. A light dusting of frost covered the grass beyond, where silver birch trees were beginning to show glimmers of life. The lawn had been mown into perfect stripes.

Looking back into the room, he saw the faded outline where a painting had once hung, or perhaps it had been a photograph. The edge was large: two metres by one-and-a-half. He felt along the seam on the wall. It was smooth at either edge but not on the frame markings. There was a rough ridge of dust and dirt. He smelled along the line. It smelt of age and decay. The image contained within it had disappeared. He could not recall what it had been.

Stumbling through a door, he came to rest in a dressing room. The units were made of dark wood and the floor was upholstered in unstained, deep piled white carpeting. He looked through some drawers, which were filled with black t-shirts, white t-shirts, black shorts, white shorts, and black socks. Hung up in a row was an array of dark suits, mostly black, with a few grey versions interspersed amongst them. The shirts on the rail were all white, black and grey. A large abstract painting aglow with reds, oranges and golds was the only discrepancy in the monochromatic space.

He stumbled out of his clothing and fitted himself into a black t-shirt and black suit. He noted the trousers were a little long and the jacket was a trifle short. He pulled a pair of black loafers from a rack of similar shoes and slipped them on. The soft leather cocooned his bare feet; they were a good, if slightly tight, fit. He plucked a set of keys from the pocket of his soiled trousers. A heavy-duty gold ring held three keys: a large one and two smaller Yale lock types. He transferred them to the pocket of the suit trousers.

His attention returned to the painting occupying one wall of the dressing space. On closer inspection he found it was deep-set in a boxed canvas and hung heavy with thick streaks of impasto paint. He reached out and touched the canvas: it was still wet. He stared at the yellow smear on his right fingertips and the small indentation his finger had left in the paint. He wiped his fingers on a white shirt sleeve hanging on the rail. A residue of the pigment remained on his skin.

Making his way back through the bedroom, he walked into a hallway. The walls were pure white. The flooring constructed of a light wood and laid in strips of perfect symmetry. On the facing wall, an enormous photograph was framed within a light box, the image a deep-focused abstract landscape. The detail was both minute and obscure. He gazed at this melancholic apparition for some time, before touching its smooth and shiny casing. Using the wound on his palm, he smeared blood in an arcing movement from the lower left to upper right. The photograph's luminosity continued to shine through the red tint left by his bloodied hand.

A floating wooden staircase wound itself around the wall. He followed it to the lower floor where the hallway was more open and airy, with generous light filtering in from outside. He found himself surrounded by open glazing and bare walls. The room held only a pair of modernist club chairs, one blue and one red, facing each other with a small glass table in between occupied by a chess board, the pieces ranged across rank and file in the midst of battle.

Sitting on the blue chair, he picked up the white king and put it to his mouth, where he bit down hard on it. He pulled it through his teeth, scraping the coating, and spat the debris onto the board. It resembled one of those chocolate mice he had purchased in a baker's shop as a child. He slipped the black king into his breast pocket and stared across at the red chair. It refused to engage him in debate. He knelt in front of the chair and felt along the seat join. The material was a finely woven wool; its smell was neutral.

He turned to a large mirror on the opposite wall. Moving towards it, he looked for his reflection but didn't recognise anything. There was a dark suit, a gash on the face, short hair and green eyes. He fixed on the image of the chairs. There were no mouths, there was no commentary.

The floor was concrete and had the same buffed effect as the walls. He placed his face upon it. It was warm and tactile. He noticed a few small, brown leaves in the corner; they smelled of the autumn. He thought about pulling them from their branches and scattering them into the fast-flowing river. He tasted them. They were dry and acrid. He spat them out. A piece of limpid vegetation stuck to the glass pane. He dragged his mouth along the seamless fibre of his jacket sleeve.

A doorway took him into an open living space. The flooring was made of deep, dark wood and there was a long, dark grey L-shaped sofa in one of the corners. Scattered amid the remaining space were black leather chairs and two large rugs, one thick and one sleek. There was no television in the room, only a slick minimal music system and speakers. At the farthest end of the room stood a high-gloss, black, baby grand piano. There were assorted tables, made of glass and wood, and one which was made of polished steel.

He noticed a tall sculpture in the centre of the room. It was formed of different colours which twisted and melted together. He moved towards it and felt all around it. The sculpture was cold and hard. Its appearance changed the closer the eye came to it. The long stretches of consistent colours, obvious from a distance, became all of a sudden made up of thousands of different hues merged together.

He pushed the large piece forcefully onto the ground. It landed with a loud crash. He then sat on the floor and pushed it along several centimetres with his feet. The sculpture scraped across the wooden flooring, taking the polish with it. He pressed his face to the artwork, smelling and licking it. The material construct was metal painted in enamel. He lay his head some distance from it, his face resting on the floor.

The sculpture warped in his vision. It cracked open slightly and mouthed the words, 'I am formless. You are formless.' After which it withered into itself once more. He waited for a time then moved towards it. His hands grappled and groped their way around it in an attempt to find the entrance. It wouldn't open. He tried desperately to prise the twisted mess apart. It would not give. His fingernail bled along a crease. He watched as the blood trickled to a halt then he rubbed it into the substance until it dried and hardened into an insignificant blemish on the impenetrable skin.

He took the chess piece from his pocket and began to chisel it into the hardened surface of the multiform. The king's head became decapitated and rolled along the floor until it came to rest under the piano.

He finally clambered to his feet, where he pulled down his suit trousers and his shorts before squatting above the contorted, painted lump of metal on the floor. He squeezed hard but nothing came out. He pushed his hand up into his anus and smeared blood from his fingertip inside. The same hand was wiped clean on the toppled art piece.

He lifted the sculpture back into its designated space in the room. It looked exactly as it had before his intervention. The light still glistened: the colours remained cavernous. The glass curtain which formed the outer wall of the living space had the hint of a blue tinge to it. Was it morning after all? A frosted light cast across the room and onto the facing white wall. He gazed at the projection playing on the blank surface.

He walked towards it and felt along its smooth, blemish-free texture. He placed his dry tongue against the cool whiteness and began to lick it hungrily. The condensation glistened for a moment before spiriting itself away, back into the lungs of the wall. His eyes wandered through the remorseless blankness of his immediate horizon, his right eye jammed into the plaster.

There was another picture missing. A slight film of dust was outlined by the new light. At the edge of this ethereal frame was the merest trace of ochre pigment. He moved cautiously towards it. He examined it before picking at it with his left hand. He received a chip of plaster work in his palm. He smelled it then tasted it. He could sense nothing from it. It was odourless and neutral. The plaster sample pierced a hole in his gum, which started to bleed. He spat the blood at the wall. Where once an artwork had hung now sat globules of brownish spit in the centre of an empty, rectangular form. He used his tongue to distribute the viscera into an exciting pattern.

He inched farther and farther away from the wall, cautiously viewing the developing ephemera on the white space. He struck his back into the large sculpture and turned swiftly to face it down. Its colours danced against his retina. He bit into the steel. Somewhere in his mouth, a tooth fractured. There was not the merest hint of material displacement on the structure. It appeared taller now than he had first encountered it as being. He tried to push it over; it would not budge. It was much heavier now than it had first seemed. He was overcome by a feeling of absolute density. The art piece was monstrous, indefinable and impenetrable. It had consumed the entire room and was crushing him against the banally pristine walls. The glass doors billowed out at their seams as they stretched to make room. The sculpture seemed to be devouring all the space surrounding him, taking all the air. He panted, he gasped, then choked, and finally succumbed to its domination, collapsing unconscious on the floor.

CHAPTER 2

It was the leg of the table which first came into view. It appeared contorted and snake-like under the plateau of the glass top. He contemplated the wood grain. He wanted to reach out and touch it, but his legs were trapped. The now inert sculpture rested heavily on top of his feet. He kicked and struggled, using his arms to pull his legs free. It took several minutes of tiresome exhortations before he managed to wrestle his feet from under its metal mass.

Sitting on the hard wood flooring, panting, he viewed the contorted painted structure at his feet. A manufactured thing, created by human hands. The culmination of unlimited resources: history, culture, art, time, energy, memory, and, of course, money. It had spoken to him and it had vanquished him.

He turned his body 180 degrees and kissed the sculpture, tenderly at first and then passionately. He licked the surface, polishing its edges, colours, sheen, until his already tender tongue was dry and numb. He clumsily rid himself of his trousers and pants. He rubbed his penis against the cold, hard surface. He wanted the mouth to open once more and devour his cock, his body, his soul.

The enamelled skin would not give. His dick could not harden. It was flaccid and raw from the attempted penetration. He lay on the rug, exhausted and expended from his exertions.

The weave of the carpet rippled slightly in a mild draft. He witnessed his spit forming in a lazy drool on the woollen surface. He stared at his broken fingernail. One half was deep red, the other a warm pink. They were separated by the crust of dark blood which linked the living and the half-living tissue alike.

He tried to recall the last time he had slept. Had he gone to bed the previous evening? Who had he slept with? He often slept alone, but rarely at the weekends. He sensed that it was Sunday. He could always divine a Sunday from other days. There was a kind of ennui that swept over everything on Sundays, tainting them with a smear of melancholic extract. The rhythms of the world slowed their tempo and missed some notes: all the important ones.

Sleep would be the cure. The shudder of alienation would dissolve in the unconscious. He never had dreams. He felt their presence, washing around in the turbulent waters of floating consciousness, but could never receive them, or know their concrete presence.

He slept a maximum of five hours per day; anything more was a waste of energy. He hated to sleep during nocturnal hours. He welcomed the darkness, with its blind rage and wilful possibilities. He was free to choose his hours and complete whatever tasks he wished in his own company.

He dressed himself carefully, concentrating completely on the task. Now he felt exhausted. He wondered if he had ever been so tired before. Had the emptiness ever felt as real as it did now? A brief skim of blue water glimmered translucently in the sunshine. He stood up, gathered his clothes around him, and staggered towards the glass doorways. He slid back three full panels of glazing to reveal a dewy sunlight. The water in the pool looked pale green again. His hand caressed the thick glass. It was fully transparent. His fingers lightly drummed on its surface. The taps were clear and strong. He pressed his nose hard into its unyielding material. It was neither hot nor cold. It was formed of a kind of limpid neutrality. He tried to breathe on it, but no breath would form. He dragged his palms around it in an oily, swirling motion. The glass remained aloof and imperious.

His lips pressed against it with disdain, they had neither spit nor inclination to attack its crystalline finish.

He pulled and pushed the doors backwards and forwards into place. Their graceful, smooth action never once deviated from its predestined trajectory.

He kicked against the doors with the sole of his right shoe then removed his left shoe and began pounding the glass, the heel acting as the head of the hammer. Neither heel nor window would yield. Eventually, he sat on the stone slabs and calmly replaced the shoe on his foot.

The water in the swimming pool was as calm as ice. He crawled on his belly towards it. The fine fibres of his suit glided along the smooth ground. When he reached the sharp edge of the pool, he plunged his face straight in. The cleansing, destructive power of chlorine punctured his tender nostrils. The murky, clouded water enveloped his sore eyes. The air hovered in his aching lungs, ready to be expelled and replenished with the hollow redemption of the liquid purity. His mouth opened noiselessly and the water poured in.

The choking and burning were immediate. The impossibility of such destructive annihilation and the absolute necessity for the act tore his head from the water. He vomited brown bile onto the side of the pool. It splashed along the grey, polished floor. His rasping cough became a dry barking, which morphed into a manic panting.

The horizon line was taken up by the streamlined green of an immaculately tended lawn. He glanced around for the gardener, but there was nobody in sight. The air was clean and quiet, as though being piped in from some sterile manufacturing plant. There were no sounds from the surrounding wildlife. He wondered if everything had been slaughtered and he was the last man on earth.

He pushed himself off his knees and surveyed the grounds. The house was a two-storey affair of concrete, glass and steel. To the right, an annexe served as a garage. He stumbled towards it, across the plush stone slabbing, noticing that the lawn tapered into an incline. There was a row of poplar trees, which followed the hill and descended into the far distance. He passed by elegantly potted palms and ferns and a dark wood sun-lounger which rested on oversized castors.

The sliding garage door was made of a mildly smoked glass. He pressed up against it and stared inside the temple-like space. The handle gave way and the door slid gently open. He wheeled the glass panel forwards and backwards, forwards and backwards, for a minute or two. He smelled the brown tinted glazing through his dribbling nostrils. He wiped his nose on the back of his hand before running it down the inside seam of the door. The glass panel was spotless and shone as though it had a warm golden tan. He pressed himself hard into its shine and rolled his face against it.

When he finally went inside, he was greeted by three immaculate white walls. The flooring was a light grey, polished concrete. In the centre of the space sat a deep green 1960s Porsche 911. The car shimmered in the pale light, supremely sepulchral and unblemished.

He stared at the headlights, which stood regimented and alert. On his knees, he genuflected towards the right-hand light. He stared dementedly at the bright white mono lens, its beam defiantly closed off. Somewhere inside, engineering had approached spherical perfection and optical precision.

As if to prove a point, his bowels cracked and a breath of rancid air permeated the pristine space. He gripped his sleeve with his fist and began to furiously wipe at the headlight, to erase the evil effulgence from its untainted skin. The tyres were black and unworn. Their dark resilience designed to tender to the submission of the rowdiest of roads. He scrabbled in his pockets and found a single gold cufflink. He bit into it and recoiled from the pain of a contaminated filling. The cufflink came down hard on the sublime painted finish of the boot. He scraped it through a layer of top paint before scuffing it around and around in a maniacal arabesque. He licked at the scrapings and dustings of paint and wax, then spat them at the windscreen. The thin vent beneath suddenly bevelled and warped. He watched with fascination as it purred softly to him, 'It is love without desire we seek'.

The newly encrusted scar on his left palm burst open from his exertions and the blood began to flow again. He dragged it along the concrete flooring, without burdening the polished texture. He clambered violently over the car, somersaulting off the back bonnet. His head cracked on the concrete and a trickle of blood seeped across the polished grey screed of the floor. He lay still, his eyes gloomily surveying the deep shadow underneath the vehicle.

To the rear of the car was a reddish leaf, hovering alone above the dark cast of the car. It was beyond the reach of his fingertips. He wondered what tree it had come from; why it had chosen to end there. His eyes closed into the hypnosis of flashing, scattered lights. He heard the roaring of a car's engine.

CHAPTER 3

He crawled around to the left side of the vehicle on his elbows and knees before raising his hand to grip hold of a metal handle. His fist felt within the hollowed dent carved out in the door. It all felt so beautifully smooth and minimally adorned. He twisted the handle around and around in his palm. He felt that his body and the car could become conjoined; his skin and the metal would solder together and he would become as perfectly formed as the vehicle parts.

He stumbled onto his knees and entered the car; the seats were an immaculate soft leather. He slid his way inside and felt along the stitched seams in the driver's seat. The cockpit felt perfectly proportioned, as though designed by an infallible computer programme. The resolutely round dials scowled at him from the dashboard. There were precisely 15,000 miles on the clock. He squeezed himself behind the steering wheel, gripping it with both hands. He stared out of the windscreen, through the garage door and down the tarmac driveway. The road curved its way around and down to the right. Brooding poplar trees started their descent in line with the sweep of the curve. The green of the lawn and the green of the trees balanced each other out perfectly. Had he witnessed this view before? He found the key in the ignition and turned it clockwise, starting the engine. Pushed into gear, the Porsche crept cautiously forward. As he lightly pressed the accelerator, it sprang frictionless from the confines of the garage and down the driveway. The tarmac was slick, bump-free, and sparkling in the mild sunlight. The Porsche rolled seamlessly along the road, just as it had straight from the production line in Stuttgart. The car appeared to be driving itself as it swept its way down the familiar, sharp and austere driveway. The poplar trees swished past as if some green splintered shadow inside a zoetrope machine. The road swam like a dark grey S-shaped river through the grounds of the house; haunted constantly by the attentively dominating, evenly spaced foliage.

It was the thirteenth poplar tree from the house. It was tall and green, with an openly western aspect. At no point during the many journeys back and forth along his driveway had Hans Zimmer expected to find his final resting place under the canopy of those branches.

His naked body lay half-covered by some lazily excavated dirt. His taut, muscular frame had greyed somewhat from his habitual Mediterranean tan. Wiped across his forehead were wisps of oil paint in a variety of autumnal hues. The damp canvas which had originally held the paint was partially draped around his neck. There were bruises and swelling where it had tourniqueted around his throat. But these marks were mere trinkets of violence in comparison to the broken piece of wooden stretcher which was protruding from his now stilled jugular vein. The blood had liquefied with the soil to form a pool of purplish sludge around the head of the corpse.

The local wildlife had shown a keen interest in this piece of carrion. A large, fat maggot was courageously squeezing its way through the core of the left eye. It had determined to colonise the central cavity of Hans Zimmer's skull before gruesomely feasting on the brain tissue at its own leisure.

Two fingers of his right hand had been gnawed off during the night. The diner had been sloppy and left the remains of the flesh scrappy, the bone protruding from the mess. There were a few bite marks and minor wounds in the middle section of the left arm, which was raised disdainfully above the ground.

Hans Zimmer's face exhibited the expressiveness of frenzied shock at his final demise. It evidenced a crudely agonising death. The body lay mutilated and appalled in a hastily dug grave. The tilled earth, as with the verminous intrusions, was freshly applied.

The lines of trees stood splendidly indifferent. The afternoon sunshine grimaced gaily over the land. The surrounding menagerie carried on its frenetic absorption in feral survival. The walls of Hans Zimmer's house stood testament to his ambition. The confines of his corpse lay unceremoniously in the soil, open prey to maggots, worms and insects.

CHAPTER 4

The ringtone was a melodious distraction of electronic beeps. It was emanating from somewhere in the glove box. Hypnotised by the line of trees banking the estate, he ignored the noise for as long as he could. A large, solid wood gate finally stopped the car in its tracks.

He fumbled in the compartment beside the dashboard and pulled out a mobile phone. The ringing had ceased. He held the thin, black slab in his palm. It was as black and opaque as the universe. It felt smooth and graceful. An alien object which had suddenly decided to manifest itself in the corporeal realm. He bit into it cautiously and removed it from his mouth by dragging it slowly across his lips. It repudiated liquid on its glistening surface. The object began singing again. He glared at the phone as the image of a painting similar to one he had witnessed in the house miraculously adorned a rectangular two-dimensional plinth at its centre. He obeyed the instructions and slid an invisible mechanism across the bottom of the image then quietly placed the phone to his right ear.

'Hans,' said the gravelly male voice on the other end, 'Hans. Is that you? It's Urs. Hans?'

'Hello,' came the monotone reply.

'Hans, is that you? Who the fuck is this?' the man named Urs demanded. 'Where the fuck is Hans? Who the fuck am I speaking to?'

'Hello,' the voice repeated.

'Is this Hans' phone? Who are you and where the fuck is Hans? This is Urs, man, and I need to talk to Hans urgently.'

'Hans?'

'Yeah man, Hans. Who are you?'

'Hans.' The name rolled around his tongue and his brain simultaneously.

'Fuck, man.' By the sound of his voice, Urs appeared

to have turned away from the phone to speak at a distance, 'I could be talking to myself here. This dumb motherfucker. Hello?'

'Hello.'

'Listen, dickhead. I need to talk to Hans urgently about a business matter. Understand?'

'Business?'

'That's right, yes, business. So where is Hans? Because that's his phone you're holding, my friend.'

'Hans' phone.'

'Listen, motherfucker, I don't know who you are or what your game is, but tell Hans to come by the apartment today. Do you understand?'

'The apartment.'

'Yes, my apartment, asshole. I'm going to text over the address in case he's forgotten it. But listen, friend. Don't you come with him. Because if you do I'm going to have to fucking kill you.'

'Kill me?'

'It's a joke. I'm joking. What, you can't take a joke? Listen, just tell Hans that Urs rang and I need to see him. Okay?'

The phone died before The Painter could respond.

Turning his attention back to the road ahead, he saw the gate before him had opened unbidden as he approached. He accepted the invitation and drove out into a desolate country road that beckoned beyond. Pressed against his chest, the phone vibrated and chirped rhythmically. A blue box containing an address appeared on the screen.

His palm felt warm against the cool industrial material of the phone. He gripped it as tightly as he possibly could. The sides of the phone dug deep marks into his skin; it began to melt in his hand, it bent and buckled before crumpling. He smashed it against his forehead until the blood gathered up in the centre of the welded crater where once the image of a painting had adorned it. He licked the blood from the encrusted bowl-like object and spattered his spit across the inside of the windscreen. Salted tears ran along his cheekbones and diluted the thick bloodstains gathered on his chin. Bubbles of froth seeped from his teeth and drooled over his knees. He gripped hold of the gearstick and tried ripping it from its socket. The instrument would not budge. The landscape before him looked frozen in space as no wind stirred in the trees. He tried to leave the car but couldn't detach himself from the seat. He wanted to examine the fields; scour them for life. Seek out the dirt in the undergrowth and climb inside its sheltering veneer.

He returned the phone to his pocket and started the car along the vacant tarmac trail. The engine opened up smoothly and the car eased itself out along the single-track country road in the sparse pastoral setting.

In a field there were lines of wheat staffs, rigid in the golden sun. In another, giant roundels of hay had been gathered up by mysteriously absent farm workers. He half-closed his eyes against the hazy blur, noting yellows and browns, rustic orange and dull green, and transferring them to a large canvas. The sky was swimming placid blue around the fringes of the windscreen. From the passenger window, a lucid sun sparkled. The black shimmer of the driveway had become an open road of a rough, uneven miasma of greys and troughs and bumps, and clods of half-eaten tarmac. The car roared along, ducking and weaving its way from the sides of ditches to the abrasions of thorny hedgerows.

He took firm hold of the driving controls and continued with his leisurely sojourn through the expansively sullen countryside. His driving veered towards the recklessly uneasy when ploughing through crossroads and around blind bends. He overtook an old green tractor slugging along a winding stretch of road with metal fence posts and wire on either side. Its vertical exhaust pumped streams of dark grey plumage into the atmosphere, leaving a funereal trail in its wake. The tractor's trailer was filled with fresh seasonal produce, packed in hard for further processing and packaging for supermarket consumption.

The Painter's journey eventually led to a crux in the road: he could either head north and deeper into the terrain of the natural landscape, or south towards the bright hinterland of the city. He spun the car out in the direction of the motorway.

The fifteen-mile journey to the peripheral roads of the urban conurbation was wedged into six even lanes of ebbing and flowing vehicles. Whenever there was a break in the view of the streams of endless traffic, there were hedges and fences and stone dykes strewn throughout the undulating horizon. Then came the small, unprepossessing buildings of the junior suburbs. The magnetic crawl of the traffic dragged all in its intensity within the realms of the arterial routes. The address on the phone spelled one destination only: a quay down by the river.

He avoided the dense heart of the city, the traffic rage and one-way streets at the heart of the planning maelstrom. The feverish discontinuity of the urban realm fed into his detached connection with external stimuli. The lamp-posts swooned down and around each turn in the road. The street signs became an overwhelming bacchanalia of banal cacophonies. The pavements and shops were an overindulgent focus of multi-coloured visions spiralling into a pixelated vortex. The sky appeared only in fits and spurts through the canopy of structures pregnant with glass and steel. The buildings appeared like mirrors turning in upon themselves and withering from their own garish adornments. The streets were a crescendo of sonic pulses: stuttering engines of buses dragged from stop to stop, honking horns and spewing revs of the taxis, of harried voices and shuffling shoes; the malignant forces of urban desecration combining to unwind its fragile truce.

The deep, sullied waters of the river glimmered in the fading remnants of the midday sun. A wisp of dark clouds began drifting in from the east. Black painted metal railings imprisoned his view of the sweeping body of water. Upstream sat the pillars of business, downstream the august seats of government and here in the middle resided Urs.

The cawing of a seagull drifted in over the murky waters enclosed by the urban sprawl. It swooped rapaciously down for some dead flotsam meandering in the current. The Painter watched as it scavenged about the stern of an old tugboat which was pulling itself towards the place where the mighty docks once stood, replaced now by expensive apartment blocks for the wealthy and well-connected.

The Painter left the car parked on the street and walked over to the black painted railings separating the populous from the black, mysterious fluid that wound its deathly way through the citadel. He wanted to dip his hands through the slim, enamelled barrier and plunge his arms deep into the cold, viscous oil slick that swerved its way through the coastal plain that had once fed an uninhibited wilderness. To scold his hands in the freezing liquid sewer swilling up against its stone and concrete prison.

The painted railings glinted in the dull sunshine. The Painter fingered along a miscreant drip, embalmed now forever in a metal tomb. He licked it gently in an attempt to revive it, move it further up the spire. His teeth dug into the metal and paint. A small fleck became disengaged and embedded itself in the inside of his bottom lip. He made no attempt to remove it. The flow of the river held his attention for a time in its majestic grip. Hypnotising him with its bleak disregard for its sprawling environment and elusive subjects.

He turned and headed towards the former warehouse that doubled as Urs' living quarters. It was built of red brick, for mercantile times now past. He came to an intercom on the wall and pressed the button. A sullen voice responded from nowhere. 'Yes? Who is it?'

'Urs phoned me,' came The Painter's laconic reply.

After a few moments the door buzzed open and he went inside. The space which greeted him was a glass atrium of double height, which let in floods of light. He wandered around a sculpture of dramatic proportions, made of steel and painted red.

He dragged a determined finger across a portion of it. Its slick, polished surface squealed in horror. There was a central staircase of unprimed metal welded together as consistently as the work of art. He trod softly upstairs and entered a large, open living area.

Sitting on an elongated black leather sofa, a middle-aged man wore a black suit and t-shirt, both of which were a little too tight. On his feet he wore a pair of black leather loafers. His hair was grey and stubbly, as was his beard. In front of him, on a glass coffee table, sat a white espresso cup and saucer. He licked brown sugar from the back of a small silver spoon. When he spoke, his voice was as dark and rough as the thick, strong espresso in his cup.

'I know you,' he announced, waving the miniature teaspoon in his direction. 'You're The Painter. We've met a couple of times. Once at a party. I can't remember which one. I'm Urs. Sit down, man.'

Urs indicated vaguely towards a chair. The Painter went to sit down.

'No, not that one,' Urs commanded. 'That one there.' He referenced a black leather chair with padded quilting. By way of explanation, Urs stated, 'That one's just for display.'

The Painter sat down.

'So what brings you to my unspeakably fashionable abode?' Urs asked.

'You phoned,' The Painter replied.

'I phoned Hans.'

'I don't know about Hans.'

'So why are you here?'

The Painter shook his head.

Urs smiled at him. 'You're represented by Francesca, yes? And that dick of a husband of hers. What are you doing with Hans' phone?'

'It was in the car.'

'Hans' car?'

'I guess so.'

'Hans is letting you drive the Porsche?'

'Yes.'

'Are you fucking him?'

'Who?'

'Hans, man. Are you fucking Hans? That guy's a sick bastard. You know he's married, right? He's got a wife and two children here in the city. He's even got a mistress. I guess he got bored and thought he'd try something new. You fuck his arse and get a Porsche. It's a good deal, man. That car's a nice ride. I was in it once. You know what kind of car I've got? Take a guess, my friend.'

The Painter didn't reply.

'A silver Rolls Royce. I even get Rudi to drive me around in it sometimes, wearing his little uniform and his cap. Have you met Rudi?'

The Painter shook his head.

'Hey Rudi,' Urs shouted towards an adjoining room, 'Rudi, come here a minute.'

A young, attractive blond male in his mid-twenties arrived in the doorway, wearing skinny jeans, a white shirt, and grey deck shoes. His face remained expressionless.

Urs gestured towards The Painter. 'This is Hans' friend, The Painter.' Neither men said anything. After a moment, Rudi silently left the room.

'He's sulking,' said Urs by way of explanation. 'I fucked a waiter two nights ago in the restaurant toilets. I was high at the time, you understand. I'll make it sweet with him again. Take him shopping. So are you fucking Hans, or what?'

'I'm not fucking anyone,' The Painter said blankly.

'It doesn't matter to me, my friend. You know what I'm saying. I've pulled some crazy fucking shit in my time. Business is business, right. He collects your work, yes?'

'I guess so.'

'He's moving into photography, though. Started collecting lots of German pieces and a few American works, too.'

'I didn't know,' The Painter replied.

Urs studied him with a sly smile. 'You know what, man, I'd take care if I was you.'

'Why's that?'

'He's going to fuck you. If he hasn't done already.' Urs smiled widely as though he had said something hilarious.

'Who's going to fuck me?'

'Hans. Hans is going to fuck you.'

'I don't fuck guys.'

'I don't mean he is actually going to fuck you. He's going to dump your work, man.'

'Dump it?'

'Don't you get it? Don't you fucking understand, man?'

'Understand what?'

'Hans is moving out of painting and into photography. Do you take photographs?'

'No.'

'Then he's going to fuck you, my friend.' Urs studied him for a moment, before opening a large wooden box on the table. He took out a long, fat cigar and unwrapped it. He placed it in a small gold guillotine and sliced off the tapered end, pausing momentarily before looking over at The Painter. Placing the cigar delicately into his mouth, and lighting it ostentatiously with a silver Zippo lighter,

Urs dramatically clipped the lighter shut before puffing on the cigar.

'These cigars,' Urs said as he contemplated the thick roll of spiralling tobacco smoke. 'they're the same ones that Winston Churchill used to smoke.'

The Painter shrugged.

'They're Cuban, of course,' Urs continued. 'I don't mind communists, though. They've never produced anything of note, well, not since the early Russians, but the Cubans make the best cigars. They've got that going for them. And the sunshine, of course, and those battered old Cadillacs those crazy fuckers run around in. It's not like the Cubans don't like good design, they just can't afford it.' He gave himself a congratulatory smile. 'These guys are always pulling shit like that.' Urs calmly reclined on the leather sofa.

'What guys?' The Painter asked.

'Dilettantes. Like your friend, Hans. How do you think these guys operate? There's no concept of aesthetic appreciation. They move quickly from one thing to the next. This is why I don't collect art.' He gestured freely with his arm around the room, by way of explanation. 'I deal in real commodities. Design. I don't dabble. I collect.' Urs flicked ash in a sculpted metal ashtray which sat on the coffee table.

'You see that chair there,' he pointed at the seat he had objected to The Painter using. 'It's an original Eames. Not one of these modern copies, but an original. Charles and Ray Eames sat in it. Tested it out. It has fucking pedigree. That, my friend, is what you call provenance.' He expelled an expansive plume of cigar smoke in The Painter's direction.

'Who are the Eames?' The Painter asked.

Urs let out a cackled roar of laughter. 'You're such a fucking peasant, man.' He paused for a moment and then continued in a more serious vein. 'But you're a talented shit. You're a creator, so you don't have to worry about such things. This is normal. This is the way of the world. I have some nice pieces by Ron Arad, Philippe Starck, more modern guys if you prefer them.'

The Painter stared at him impassively.

'So, you don't like design.' Urs looked at his cigar. 'And you don't like cigars, or you don't like the Cubans. And so, my friend, why the fuck are you here?'

'You phoned.' The Painter obliged.

'I phoned Hans.' Urs pointed out with the fat roll of tobacco.

'I don't know where Hans is.'

'You don't?' Urs eyes narrowed slightly. 'So, who does?'

'How should I know?' The Painter replied impatiently.

Urs knocked some more ash from his cigar into the ashtray. Rudi appeared from the doorway, carrying a cuboid glass tumbler with a small amount of burnt amber liquid in it. He walked silently over to the coffee table and placed the glass in front of Urs. He then disappeared back through the doorway again. Urs picked up the glass and smelled inside it before running the fluid around in the glass. He held it up to The Painter.

'Single malt from out in the islands. That's where they make the best stuff. This one's from Islay. I would be more hospitable, but I don't trust you, my friend.'

'I'm not thirsty,' The Painter said.

'Do you know why I need to speak to Hans?' Urs asked.

'No.'

'Hans has something I need. And he was going to exchange it for something I have, or rather that I can get hold of for him.'

'What's that?'

'A photograph. A good one. A Dusseldorf one.'

'In return for?'

'A contact. Contacts, in fact. In China. It's a burgeoning market and Hans knows people. People that I would like to get to know. You see, my friend, I know something that you don't.'

'Which is?' The Painter glanced distractedly around the room.

'That fifty years from now we'll all be speaking Mandarin.'

'Mandarin?'

Knowing he had his audience secured, Urs sat back. 'It's logical. It's simple evolution. The Romans, the Vikings, the Christians, Islam, the British, the Nazis, the Americans, it's all the same thing; evolution, my friend.' Urs spun his cigar around in the air. 'The wheel keeps turning. Where it will stop, nobody knows. Except this time it's going to stop in fucking Beijing, man. And to those who have the keys, goes the kingdom.'

'I don't know any Mandarin.' The Painter said as he closed his eyes with fatigue.

'And you don't know where Hans is?' Urs took a swig of his whisky.

'No.'

'In that case why don't we have ourselves a little deal?'

The Painter opened one eye. 'What kind of a deal?'

'You find Hans and sweeten him up and I'll cut you in for a slice of the pie.'

'What pie?'

'Art doesn't just move one way. It doesn't just move out of China, it also moves in. Shanghai has its collectors, too. I might be able to help you to shift some of your paintings. You're going to need a new market.'

'Why's that?'

'I'm trying to explain this to you, my friend. That dealer of yours, Francesca and her bastard husband, you can't trust them. She'll fuck you over in a second, man. In your game the latest thing is always waiting around the next corner. You know, I had acquired a certain piece Francesca wanted for one of her clients. She made me an offer and I said no. Then this crazy fucking bitch says she'll throw in a blow job. She wanted to suck my fucking cock in the middle of this party. In her Valentino dress and Prada heels.

'I told her that she wasn't my type of cocksucker and she says if I like, she can get her husband to do it instead. How can you deal with such people? This is a problem for you, my friend. Me, I don't give a shit, I don't collect art. I don't need to concern myself with individuals of this type. But you, my friend, this is your business.' Urs finished his drink and placed the glass tumbler on the table, drawing deeply on his cigar.

'Look, man, find Hans for me, bring him here, and we'll do the deal. Everyone gets to walk away a winner. Even you.'

Urs stood up and walked over to The Painter. He shook his hand and in doing so pulled him off the chair. He looked at his face. 'Rough night, my friend. You look like shit. You should go home, get a rest, get changed, then after that, find Hans. OK?' He helped The Painter to the stairs. 'You can see yourself out, yes. I need to go and make up with Rudi now. Otherwise he'll be in a sulk until Monday morning.'

The Painter began to descend the stairs. He turned around to face Urs. 'You don't know my address, do you?'

Urs let out a roar. 'What? Are you fucking with me, man? Where the fuck did you go last night? You want to know your address? I'll tell you where it is. You go up the street and turn left.' He continued laughing to himself as he moved back into the living space.

CHAPTER 5

The Painter left the building and walked back out into the street. The sky had turned slate and there was the menace of a mild drizzle in the air. He raised his head before heading over to the Porsche, feeling the sprinkle of a cool, crisp film of water sink into his skin.

A large globule of bird excrement sat in the centre of the windscreen. He gazed at its sticky, white mass before running a finger through it. A section attached itself to his fingertip. He sniffed hard at it before rubbing it around his gums, running his tongue along its traces before retching over the boot of the car. No vomit was forthcoming as he slid down the paintwork onto the cobbled road. He sat, staring at the cold grey contours of each block wedged together, before slipping his fingers between the cracks of the stones, scraping the insides of them, and pulling the dirt along into a pile at the end of each.

Through the railings he could view a small launch gliding along the water. At its helm was a middle-aged male dressed in white flannels, a polo shirt, and pastel jumper. Even from a distance, The Painter could see he had streaked highlights in his hair, well-moisturised skin, and a pair of thick black shades over his eyes. Next to him, ensconced in his arms, was a younger woman; blonde-haired, in a blue-and-white striped jumper and black cut-off trousers, ubiquitous sunglasses perched on her plastic nose.

The Painter watched the water part ways for this miniature yacht. He wished only to immerse himself in the turmoil left in the boat's wake; to death-roll in the white effervescence flowing out into the dead-eyed river. To glory and revel in the final descent into the depths of the sewage-infested swamp that swam its way around the city. The sluice of water winched its way upriver, following the vessel piloted by the perfect couple, who seemed destined for another night in Shangri-La. He gripped the car's front bumper and dragged himself onto his feet. The city felt vast and utterly impenetrable, a giant cipher bereft of all meaning. He considered visiting Urs again and trying to generate some sense of where he belonged.

Instead, he gripped the handle and pulled outwards on the door. Inside the car, he slumped onto the driver's seat. The speckled drips of drizzle hitting the windscreen contrasted heavily with the avian defecation. His fatigue seemed unbearable. The day had continued onwards, undaunted and undefeated. The Painter felt his continuance in this state was an open admission of absolute masochism. He looked at his hands, which appeared crude and wrinkled, weathered by oil paints and acrylics, rough soaps and turpentine. He raised them up to his nostrils and breathed them in. They smelled of a kind of living death, detailed in their bitter qualities mixed in with a slightly sweet and sickly rancidness from his open wounds. They smelled of an organic matter putrefying before his very eyes. He fully expected them to have decayed into calcified bone stumps by the end of the day. There was nothing to be hoped for in them anymore. The sky outside darkened further and the Porsche's interior was bathed in shadows.

The Painter seized the phone and began to sift through the contacts. On one was a photo of a painting similar to those in the house in which he had awoken. He searched for the address. It lay east of the river in an old industrial part of the city; part gentrified, part working meat-market.

He started the car engine and made for what he hoped would be home. The windscreen wipers mixed the bird excrement with the grey contaminated industrial rain water, to leave a film of grease over half the coverage of the wipers.

As the quantity of rain improved, so did his visibility. The car eased out into the lazy afternoon traffic and almost glided unimpeached through the twenty-minute journey to its destination. The streets surrounding the four-storey brick building were strewn with debris from the debaucheries of the night before. Takeaway cartons and empty bottles had run into the streets which well-dressed types with dogs, out for a Sunday stroll, carefully picked their way around. The market close by was dead to the day. The streets seemed elegantly grubby, as though by design rather than neglect.

He parked the car and stumbled out. On his way to the front door he picked up an errant beer bottle. He began to peel the label from it, tearing the strips from the smooth brown glass before tossing them onto the pavement. He tired of his efforts and duly smashed the bottle against the wall. It crashed open upon the bricks with a thud before scattering over the paving slabs. He walked over and stood above the crystals before stooping low for a better view, admiring the dashes of random patterns he had created. He knelt down on the cold floor and held his breath. The noise of his heart crumpled into a ceaseless thudding in his eardrums. He squeezed hard into his stomach with both arms before gasping and spluttering his way back into a full breathing rhythm.

He slapped his face twice, hard, before spitting on the shards. He picked one glass splinter off the ground and held it gently in his hand, like the petal of a rose. Then he crushed it with malevolence into the palm of his hand. He took the streaming blood and, using his thumb, drew a line along the pavement.

He got to his feet, marched over to the car, and dried the blood from his hand on the front left wing. Across the street were pallets and empty boxes, remnants of the last shift at the meat-market. Two soiled teenagers passed by in full football kit; tired, solemn and homeward-bound, in apparent defeat.

The Painter turned his attention to the large wooden

door, at the centre of the building. He walked up the three steps guarded with metal railings at either side. He felt the black enamel paintwork on the left-side railing. It was smooth to the touch, with some droplets of rain glistening on it, but there were no runs in the brushwork for him to fondle delicately. He lay his left cheek upon the railing. A sharp sting of cold hit his face, shocking his nerve endings and causing a minor reflex reaction of a brief tremor to pass through his head. He stared at the double-sided wooden door, standing awkwardly gallant in the ruinous street. He took the set of keys from his pocket and tried the largest first. It fitted the lock perfectly and with two clicks to the left he was inside the building.

CHAPTER 6

The Painter was greeted by a large entrance hall; the floor made up of a geometric mosaic of monochrome tiles. The stairway swept upwards to the left and downwards to the right. The individual steps themselves were laid with black-and-white tiling on both the vertical and horizontal axis. The banister on the stairway was made up of a wooden handrail on top of rows of metal bars painted once more in the ubiquitous black enamel paint.

He cautiously mounted the stairs. He dragged his left hand along the smooth varnished finish of the handrail. He then pushed it forwards and began to drag himself wearily to the next landing. A young woman came skipping down the stairs. Her blonde hair was swept back into a tight ponytail. She wore stretched black shorts and a black sports vest covered with a zipped, white hooded top. Her feet were adorned with short white socks and white running shoes with an elaborate pink swish. In spite of her earphones and his physical state of disrepair, she smiled at him politely and said 'Hi' before swiftly dancing down the remaining steps and out into the street.

The Painter watched the door close after her, with an equally polite thud, before continuing his ascent to the first floor. At the landing he pushed his way through the safety-glass-panelled, wooden-framed fire door. The corridor was a darkened space with only a basic glow emanating from two emergency lights. He came to the first door on his left and pulled out his keys once more. He tried the Yale lock with the first key, which didn't fit, and moved on to try the second, which did.

Through the door was a large studio space. On the opposite wall, four large windows filtered in vast amounts of light. Each window displayed twelve individual panes of glass. The upper halves of the middle two windows were open at 45-degree angles. Screwed into the wall were four solid bars for each window. The windows were painted white, the bars black. The floor was made of varnished wooden planks. Around the entire circumference of the studio were sheets of heavy-duty white paper neatly taped together in a partially successful attempt to protect the floor. Splashes of coloured paints were scattered across the exposed wooden boards.

In front of the left wall stood two large wooden easels, currently unoccupied. By the studio door was a large white industrial-sized sink incorporating a solid wooden unit. Within the sink and unit were various metal pots filled with paint brushes and an array of other implements. They were steeping in vast quantities of turpentine, which lent the studio an oxidising air. Next to the sink unit were a dozen canvases lined up. Several were large pieces, at a couple of metres in length, some were medium-sized, and the rest smaller affairs. The essentially whitewashed walls were dotted with various tester blobs for a vast palette of colours and hues. At the opposite wall, underneath the windows, were a series of stainless steel tables laden with tubes of oil paint, bottles of thinners and mixers, paint brushes of all descriptions, and a plethora of windscreen wipers, floats, trowels, scrapers, and pointing tools.

A desk sat in front of the wall, on the right, with a drawing table. To the side was an open cupboard filled with an assortment of paper, pencils, charcoals, chalks and pastels. Pinned to the wall above the drawing desk were a few densely-drawn abstract pictures. To the right side of the wall was another door. The drawing desk had a small, flexible black lamp clamped onto it. Over by the easels was a six-foot-high tripod with two separate lamps attached. The lighting above was provided by three banks of large, swinging pendant lights.

The cloying smell of oil paint clung to the entire space; the open windows provided a much-needed respiratory relief. The Painter unhooked a towel which was hanging up next to the sink. It was light purple in colour and damp to the touch. It had splashes of oil paint encrusted on it. He bit down into one and began to chew at the cotton rag. He burrowed his face into it and drank in its pungent aroma of oils, turpentine, and industrial-strength hand cleaner. He pulled the towel away and held his head over the sink. Using his right thumb, he chipped at a piece of paint stuck to the enamel bottom. He held the scraping of pigment close to his eye before placing it on his tongue. He then spat the piece into the plughole.

The Painter closed his eyes and leaned his head on the side of the sink. The white ceramic surface was smooth and cool. He rubbed his head back and forth along it. He gripped hold of the cold tap and cupped his left hand underneath, then gently splashed water onto the back of his neck. The Painter took the towel and dried himself. He rubbed the towel all over his body until he smelled like his studio; he had fused and merged his identity with it, 'You are me and I am you.'

The Painter turned towards the inner door, which led to a second room as large as the studio. The first part was given over to the kitchen area. There was a fridge, a combined oven and grill, and cupboards. Under the window, a sink sat next to a complex and well-used coffee machine. An island unit held a stainless steel four-burner hob and a knife block containing six steel chef's blades. At the other end of the island was a breakfast bar with three stools placed neatly beneath it.

The central space in the room was given over to a living area. On the back wall, beneath the window, a three-seater, black leather sofa had parallel chrome bars running around the sides and the back. There was a black leather armchair, of the same design, and a large, silver, angle-poise lamp sat to the left of the sofa. In front was a square chrome-and-glass coffee table.

A bureau with three large drawers held an old-fashioned dial telephone, with a wood-veneered, tape-driven answering machine. A reporter's pad and black biro pen were perched next to the phone. On the opposite wall, an old 1970s stereo system sat on top of a wooden unit containing a large collection of vinyl records.

At the back of the room, the bedroom area held a double bed covered in white sheets, next to which was a small bedside table with a lamp and a book sitting upon it. To the side of the bed was a series of shelves containing a great number of books. These reached close to the apex of the high ceiling. A five-rung ladder was on hand for gaining access to the uppermost books. There was also a long metal locker and a four-drawer metal filing cabinet.

There was a doorway on the wall opposite the windows, towards the back of the space. The Painter edged his way towards this. He looked into a short corridor with a door on either side. He tried the door to the left. It led into a bathroom containing a WC and a sink. In the right corner, attached to the ceiling, was a large metal shower head. Under the shower was a plughole. The entire room was tiled with a mosaic of grey on the floor and terracotta on the wall. There was one window above the sink with a mirrored bathroom cabinet screwed to the wall next to it. On top of the toilet was a roll of paper. None of it looked familiar.

The Painter wandered back through to the living space. He felt around the area, trying to position the bearings of his memory.

CHAPTER 7

The Painter opened the metal locker. Hanging inside were three identical black suits. At the bottom was a pair of polished, black leather shoes. The top drawer of the filing cabinet held half-a-dozen t-shirts, all white or black. The second drawer held four pairs of jeans in both blue and black. In the third drawer were several pairs of black shorts with a white elasticated band at the top, stitched with the name 'Calvin Klein'. In the bottom drawer were around a dozen pairs of black socks.

The Painter walked over to the bedside table and picked up the book which lay perched on it: *Steppenwolf* by Hermann Hesse. He leafed carelessly through the book. He brought it up to his nostrils. It was a yellowed old paperback edition and smelled dusty and ancient, as though born into, and destined for, another time and place. He flicked the pages back and forth in the hope they would converse with him. Form a mouth and annunciate. The pages simply whirled open and shut with a flick of his thumb and forefinger.

He moved to the bookshelves. Many of the spines on display suggested they were about artists and art movements: Caravaggio, Picasso, Monet, Da Vinci, Giotto, Giacometti, Delaunay, Titian, Rothko, Warhol, Duchamp, Miro, Matisse, Beuys, Raphael, Richter, Rembrandt, Courbet, Manet, El Greco, Bacon, De Kooning, Klein, Motherwell, the Surrealists, the Orphists, the Italian Renaissance, the Dutch Masters, the Cubists, Conceptualism, Pop Art, the Dadaists, the Situationists, the Abstract Expressionists, Ancient Rome, Ancient Greece, African Sculpture, Japanese Noh Theatre, the avant-garde in European literature, Wordsworth, Eliot, De Quincey, the Marquis de Sade, Rimbaud, Mallarmé, Byron, Shelley, Hamsun, Mann, Melville, Dickens, Brecht, Pirandello, Strindberg, Ruskin, Stanislavski.

He drummed his fingers along the spines of the books. He knocked on them with his knuckles. There was no reply.

He went over to the sofa and sat down. The leather creaked into place around him. He felt its clean, smooth shine. The Painter dragged his damaged palm across the glass table-top, leaving a residue of sweat, dirt and blood on its surface. He dropped to his knees and tried to remove it by licking the table clean, but it just smeared even more. He let a long string of spit land in the centre of the table, then used his left index finger to move it around and around, pushing it out to the edges of the table itself.

He sat up on the sofa and leaned his head back, closing his eyes against the late afternoon sunshine which was filtering in from the long windows behind him. He beat down hard with his fist on the leather seating. He dug his fingers hard into his palm and could feel the blood well up in his hand. He breathed uneasily as he cried.

The Painter carried himself back through to the studio once again and walked straight up to one of the large canvases. Inspired, he pushed his bleeding hand in random strokes across the surface of the tight white material. Dribs and drabs of dark, muted pigment appeared as uncontrolled darts and fits in the massed blankness. He pushed his forehead aggressively into the stretcher, bending part of the canvas inwards. He stood back from the work, in contemplation of it, before kicking a hole clean through it.

The Painter fell to the floor and sat cross-legged, holding his face in his hands. The colours flickered around in his mind: languid oranges, reds and greens, forming and unforming in instantaneous bursts of lifelessness. The animalistic tinge of blood filled his nostrils. He breathed in and out deeply for several minutes. When he lowered his hands, opened his eyes, and glanced around the room, the dying light of the early evening was dancing in deep yellow shadows.

He walked through to the kitchen and opened the fridge. Inside were two unopened bottles of Pol Roger champagne and nothing else. In the freezer was a three-quarters-full bottle of Finlandia vodka, a bag of ice cubes, and a small Tupperware box filled with frozen slices of lemon and lime. He looked in one of the cupboards and discovered some tins of tomatoes, mushroom soup, and baked beans. In the cupboard next to that were crockery and glasses. The Painter helped himself to a glass tumbler, into which he placed two slices of lemon and lime apiece before applying a healthy slug of vodka. He sipped the clear, cloying liquor, pushing it around his tongue and teeth before swallowing heavily. It burned its way down his oesophagus and into his stomach. A drowsiness entered his system as the alcohol sluiced around his body. To counter the drink, he crashed through another cupboard to find a small pan in which to cook a tin of beans. He turned on a gas ring but didn't light it immediately, pausing to smell the noxious aroma given off by the fuel. It evoked the image of a slow death: pupils dilating, nerve ends twitching, an atrophy setting in, the body unable to resist its own demise. The flames sparked up with a momentary intensity before settling back down to a constant warmth.

The Painter simmered the beans until the excess sauce had boiled away and a sticky mush remained. He ate straight from the pot, using the red spatula he had used to stir the beans. They emitted the quality of a sweet, salty paste, mashed in with tender, melting husks. He gagged them down his throat, using the heavy vodka as a combustible companion. His stomach barely held the leaden partnership together. His gut heaved and swayed before being assuaged by another hefty soaking of booze.

He placed the half-burned pot to soak in the sink, along with hot water and washing-up liquid, of which he also rubbed a little around in his hands. The smell created a damp anaesthetic resonance that The Painter found to be a minor comfort. He wiped his hands on a nearby tea towel without rinsing away the soapy residue first. He smelled his hands again several times as he made his way to the answering machine.

A red light flashed furiously on the top of the machine. He pressed the play button and was advised that he had two new messages. The first was from a woman who identified herself as Emily, who was phoning from his gallery to advise him of an up-and-coming piece dedicated to his work in the latest copy of *Art and Culture* magazine. The piece was by the eminent critic Dan Smithson. The second call was from Dan Smithson himself, advising The Painter to meet him at The Duck and the Whore pub that evening.

The Painter rolled the names around in his mouth, eliciting a vague response of hazy physical impressions and for Emily a secondary sexual arousal. Had he fucked her? There was no evidence of female domesticity anywhere within the studio complex. It was a purely male environment. As he scanned his surroundings he was partially unconvinced that there was actual evidence of his own existence in the apartment. The essence of the place felt part of him and yet at the same time somehow separate. It held the feel of an approximation of processed information rather than of a real lived experience.

The Painter responded to the inclement existential atmosphere by fixing himself another vodka, which went down a lot more smoothly than the previous had, having some half-masticated beans to bounce off.

Wandering back into the atelier, he tried to get a sense of the man who inhabited the space. The man who created his illusory world in the confines of those walls. When had he last been there? It was certainly his world, even if it remained entirely distant from him. The brushes were his. The canvases were his. The drawings were his. He recognised them as such. It all felt at once so familiar and at a remove so unfamiliar.

Emily, he knew, Dan Smithson, he knew, and Hans he knew. He hadn't remembered Urs, but Urs had remembered him, or had at least claimed to know him. Urs was not a man to be trusted, of course, but perhaps Dan Smithson was. He would much rather be meeting Emily.

He walked over to the oil paints and picked out a cadmium yellow. He unscrewed the top and squeezed some onto the damaged canvas dowsed with his blood. He pushed his nose down close to the visceral smear of pigmented oil. He sniffed at the paint twice in long, drawn-out inhalations. He began smelling it with a hurried, exaggerated excitement. His nostrils pulled at the scent again and again, gulping down its intense odour. He thought of Emily. Short raven hair. Deep red lips. Green lynx eyes and a slightly cruel stare. He thought of a tall frame. A slender waist and full breasts. Firm calves and long thighs. He thought of a tight arse, pushed out slightly. He thought of the soiled canvas. He thought of dripping, unctuous paint.

He sniffed ecstatically at the yellow cadmium oil. He kept on sniffing as he pulled his penis out from his trousers and began masturbating and he kept on sniffing as he ejaculated onto the canvas. He gathered up some residual semen in his hand, stood back and threw it at the yellow paint stain. He then grasped hold of a palette knife and worked the pigmented, biological concoction into the fine weave of the cotton surface.

After some deftly swirling distractions, The Painter dropped the soiled palette knife to the floor. It hit the wood blade-down and stood erect in its grains. He stared down at the knife before pressing his heel on top of it. The knife, unable to bear the stress, flipped over and nicked his right ankle. He kicked it angrily across the studio floor.

The Painter stumbled back into the living area and went

over to the answering machine. He rewound the two messages he had received and played them back again. He listened attentively to Emily's cool, professional voice and to Dan Smithson's harried one, which seemed to alternate somewhere between pleading and commanding. He took the mobile phone from his pocket and looked up the address of The Duck and the Whore pub, adding it to the phone's satellite navigation system.

He rolled up his right trouser leg to reveal a small, shallow gash on his ankle. He then took the half-drunk vodka on the breakfast bar, slung it down his throat, and went back through to the studio. He glanced around once more before exiting via the door through which he had entered less than an hour ago.

The corridor outside the studio was dark; only an emergency exit light glowed on the end wall. There was a kind of grave silence, as though the city outside had been eradicated. The thud of a door, swinging shut on its industrial hinges, broke the stillness.

The Painter exited into the stairway, deftly lit by way of fluorescent lighting. He ran his hand along the wall as he clambered down. Rubbing his palm around and around the heavy cream-and-yellow paintwork.

The street outside the building was quiet, but across the road the night was starting to get underway. Vans had begun to arrive and carcasses were being processed. He watched the whitened rib cages and the deep scarlet undercarriages of sawn-up cows. The freshly skinned pigs were a mortuary texture of greying pink. The waft of death drifted up the street. It smelled of constipation and calcified decay; rigor-mortised ennui and the rendered fat of anti-matter.

The Porsche had a plastic envelope stuck to the windscreen. The Painter tore it from the glass and ripped it open. The piece of paper inside warned him of an imposed fine for a traffic violation. He held it up against a streetlamp, examining it closely, then tossed it into the gutter. At his feet were the offending yellow, parallel lines. He ran his left foot along them in turn, feeling each bump and blemish. He stared up at the darkening sky, already orange-hued from the city's lights.

Sniffing heavily, he pulled phlegm through his nose and into his mouth. He swirled its mucous rancidity around his palette before spitting hard into the road markings. A long globule of spit centred itself on the inner stripe. It clung, limpet-like, bridging a crack in the paint's encrusted dilapidation. He thought of peeling the fluorescent marking from the grey/brown tarmac and lugging it upstairs to glue onto a canvas. It didn't belong in the realm of the corporeal world, its ragged beauty elevated into the realms of the gazed-upon.

The Painter climbed inside the Porsche and turned the engine over. He laid the mobile phone on his lap. The city seemed both serene and malevolent in the burgeoning night. The streets protruding with a darkness and mystery missing from the harsh blur of daylight. He fumbled around for the switch to engage the lights. Once on, they served to highlight the scree of grease coating the windshield. He wiped an index finger down the inside of the glass, adding a new mark. Then he swung the car out on the road and followed the phone's directions.

The journey took him on a downward spiral into the heart of the urban beast. Past the empirically laid-out grand squares, the towering monoliths of commerce, the bric-a-brac streets and the decayed social housing. He followed the automated directions that took him to the hip side of town, filled with jaded, violent youth, up-and-comers, and meritocratic weekend slummers.

He pulled up outside the grand edifice of The Duck and the Whore bar. Its large painted sign, hanging on the side of the building, featured a cartoon of a busty maiden replete in black bra, red knickers and black fishnet stockings. To the lower left of this comely wench was a menacingly lascivious duck with a large, phallic-shaped bill. Underpinning the grotesque scene was an illustration of an idyllic, rural setting.

The Painter turned off the car's lights and engine and emerged onto the pavement. A poorly dressed middle-aged man staggered along the street, stopping briefly to inspect The Painter and the Porsche with equal interest, before continuing on his peripatetic wanderings through the city. An attractive young couple holding each other's hands bobbed and weaved around the drunken man before skipping into the pub.

The Painter stood for a moment, contemplating the large, shiny windows of the bar. They were all frosted white and laid out in a line along the wall, like some magnificent, minimalist installation. He walked up to one of the windows, pressed his face against it, and spied the dark, cavernous interior on the other side. The glass was slightly rough-feeling and he rubbed his stubble around it. He tried to view his reflection, but it was just a shadowy spectre on the blank pane. The glass finally smoothed over and interceded with a cool whisper in his ear, 'I am blood made flesh.' The wall felt suddenly concave and detached from the overall structure. The Painter imagined floating away attached to it. Sailing through the night, as though on some magic carpet ride in a children's fable. He tried to grip hold of the windowsill in case the wall took off, but it remained stagnant.

CHAPTER 8

Eventually steadied, The Painter prised himself from the window and entered the building through the same doorway the young couple had used. Inside, it was larger than he had anticipated, and less crowded. To the side wall, where the windows hung, were banquettes of red leather seating. He noticed the view to the outside world was obscured by the glass as it only reflected inwards. It gave the building an expansive appeal. Strung along the central walkway were glass-and-chrome tables, with slung black leather chairs. The bar took up most of the opposite side of the building. It was light and flashy, with red leather bar stools ranged all the way along it. A neon sign indicated the restaurant was up the plush, red-carpeted, sweeping stairway.

Sitting on his own at the bar was a man in his mid-forties, wearing a black pork pie hat with a dark band around it. He wore faded rolled-up jeans and a pair of grey, canvas deck shoes with no socks. On top he wore a blue-and-white striped t-shirt and a navy jacket. His face held a pair of black, thick-rimmed, circular glasses. He was halfway down a tall, elongated glass of lager. He turned to view The Painter as he approached him.

Dan Smithson struck out his hand in The Painter's direction and said, 'Hey man, grab a pew.'

The Painter limply took Dan's hand, dropped it and pulled himself onto the adjoining bar stool.

The critic assessed The Painter's condition through his thick lenses. 'What the fuck happened to you, man?' he asked, half laughing, 'You look like shit.'

The Painter simply shrugged. Dan returned, smiling, to his beer. 'Well, I hope she was worth it.'

The barman approached The Painter and asked, 'What's your pleasure, sir?'

The Painter looked up at him. He was young, in his

mid-twenties; thick brown hair, regular tan, clean-shaven, without jewellery or tattoos; in other words, a pro. 'I'll have a vodka.'

'Any preference?'

'Finlandia, if you have it.'

'I certainly have,' the barman exclaimed, pleased to have identified a connoisseur as he went to fix the drink.

'Just ice, lime and lemon,' The Painter called after him.

The barman nodded his assent.

'So amigo, how's tricks in the fast world of canvas hangers?' Dan looked The Painter in the eye, as The Painter continued to watch his drink being made. Dan pressed him, 'You're not sore about that last review, are you? I've talked you up this time, well up. It could be a nice little earner for you. Sell lots of paintings out of it. Not that you've got any problems in that regard. Talented shit, aren't you?'

Dan returned to his glass and threw a large gulp down his throat. The barman brought The Painter his vodka. Smithson indicated the drink. 'Stick that on my tab, would you?'

'Of course, sir,' the barman replied, moving on to his next mark.

The critic looked around the bar. 'It's always dead in here on a Sunday night, they make all their money from Thursday to Saturday. All they get in here on a Sunday night is the well-off students.' He indicated towards a group of late teens at a banquette in the corner. 'Happy to spend mummy and daddy's hard-earned money on over-priced, poxy cocktails.'

The group were drinking a pink concoction in champagne flutes, poured from a large glass jug in the centre of the table. 'Look at them,' he continued, warming to his subject, getting more annoyed. 'They wouldn't know Buckfast from Chateau le Cunt. I'll have to go and review their work at the end of the year, see if I can't spot a Hirst or an Emin amongst them. Or maybe even a younger version of you.' He sneered, turning his annoyance towards The Painter. 'Remember how I kickstarted your career all those years ago?' He added in a more reflective manner, 'And my own, for that matter.' Smithson looked into his drink. 'You were a good painter back then. You could even have become a great one. Until you started knocking out that shtick you do now. But they all lap it up, don't they?'

The Painter looked at him, confused. 'Who?'

'Your select band of clients,' Dan Smithson answered coldly.

The Painter took a drink of his vodka.

Smithson continued. 'I'm sorry. I'm feeling slightly bruised at the moment. Maybe I'm having one of those mid-life crises. You know the ones, when you question your very right to existence and everything you've wasted your fucking life doing.' Dan looked to The Painter for an indication of empathy.

The Painter watched as a gentle bead of perspiration ran down the side of Dan Smithson's tall glass. He pushed out a finger to catch it, lifted it up, and placed it on his tongue. It felt cool and purged of all impurities.

The critic watched him, bemused. 'Are you okay, man? You seem a little off kilter tonight. Did you get in fight with someone?'

Dan gripped The Painter's right wrist, caught by the injury in its palm. 'What happened to your hand? That looks like a bad gash you've got there.'

'It's nothing,' The Painter snapped as he wrestled his hand back and used his finger to stop another drip of moisture running down Smithson's beer glass.

'You remind me of John Mills in that scene from *Ice Cold in Alex*. The one where he plays an alcoholic. Have you seen it?'

The Painter continued to watch the fresh trickles run

down the cold glass.

'You're not an alcoholic, are you?' The critic laughed. 'Still, it's good for your image, huh? I bet they lap that shit up in their whirligig round of endless parties. Those clients of yours.'

The Painter stared at the critic. 'What clients?' he finally asked.

Dan Smithson shouted out from his stool. 'Barman, more drinks s'il vous plait?' He drained the rest of his lager, then smacked his lips together in an exaggerated fashion.

The Painter felt along the smooth leather of his seat, its tight, unyielding weave. A feeling of luxury and craftsmanship. He dug his nails into the covering as hard as he could. He tried to tear at it, seeking to penetrate the underside of the material.

'I need to ask you a favour, man.' Dan Smithson turned to The Painter, slightly ashen, his voice wobbling. 'I'm in a spot of trouble.'

'What kind of trouble?' The Painter asked.

'I've got a debt I have to repay rather sharpish.'

'A debt? What kind of debt?'

'The worst kind of debt: a gambling debt. To the worst kind of collector of debts. This crazy bastard called The Siberian.'

'The Siberian?'

'That's what he calls himself. I don't know what his real name is, probably Vlad the Impaler or some sort of shit like that. Needless to say, he isn't happy about this debt. Neither its size, nor the amount of time it's taking me to pay it back.'

'How much is it?'

Dan took a large sip of his beer. 'Fifty fucking thousand. That's a year's salary to me. I can't pay it.'

'So don't pay it.'

Dan Smithson looked at him and smiled without

humour. 'You're a real funny motherfucker, you know that? What's it like up in that rarefied atmosphere? I'm not one of your rich flunkies, all diamond tiaras and fox furs. I don't have a pot to piss in. Why do you think I owe some gangster bookmaker so much money?'

'He's a gangster?'

'Of course he's a fucking gangster. Who else lends out that kind of line of credit to an art critic?'

'What happens if you don't pay?' asked The Painter, only mildly interested.

'He fucks me up, that's what. Do you know what he says he's going to do if I don't get him the money this week?'

'What?'

'He says he's going to crucify me.'

'Crucify you?' Intrigued, The Painter waited to hear more.

'Yes. He actually said he's going to crucify me. He says he's going to nail my hands and feet down to the floorboards in my own loft space. Can you imagine how painful that would be? Nails through the flesh. He says you can wriggle yourself free eventually, but you have to pull the nails right through your skin and bones. It can take days to do, apparently. You lose buckets of sweat in the process, through sheer exertion. He says that he'll be kind and attach a dirty old rag to my mouth so that I won't disturb my nice neighbours with my screams.'

'Is he serious?'

'Well, why don't we just wait and find out? Won't that be fucking fun? Yes, I'll just sit here for the next week and see if he comes to collect me. Then I'll tell him my friend here, the great artist, thought that he was probably joking. Larking about like we were in the playground together or something. Yes, he's fucking serious, man. Of course he's serious. He's some kind of a Russian gangster. He's probably got lots of tattoos to show for his troubles. He's probably also been doing this shit since before he could crawl. Hanging cats from trees and watching them struggle to get free of the noose while it tightens around their cute little scrawny necks. Who knows how psychopaths get their kicks? I wrote a review once, about a sculpture that I thought was awful. It sold for a lot of money to one of these shadowy types you probably have dealings with far more than me. Well, I wrote this piece excoriating it, in a blue chip, American art journal. So I'm sitting in the bar of my sweet little boutique hotel in Manhattan and this guy sits up next to me. He's burly, but nicely dressed in a three-piece grey silk suit. He orders his drink, a nice glass of Rioja, and sits quietly sipping it. Then he turns to me and asks if I'm the critic that wrote the article calling this piece of sculpture an over-priced, polished turd, dumped out of a crap artist's arse. So I come over all coy and laugh and then say, yeah, that was me. This guy, the one in the nice suit, with the nice wine, tells me this piece I wrote upset a friend of his, a collector, the guy who actually bought the hideous fucking thing. It turns out this cultured art collector is some sort of Mexican businessman and the last journalist that pissed him off was found, flayed alive, with his skin sewn onto a mannequin and thrown into a river with some witty epithet tagged onto it. They played a game of football with his head. They wore steel-toe-capped safety boots and one of them even managed fifty keepie-uppies with it, before sending it to the victim's wife as a present for their tenth wedding anniversary. Those demented fuckers are off the scale down there. This Siberian, on the other hand, is merely going to crucify me.'

'Why did they sew his flayed skin to a mannequin?' The Painter asked, puzzled.

'Because they're fucking headbangers, man. They're letting everyone know that they're capable of anything. How humiliating and disgusting would it be to know you were going to end up with your skin being stitched to a fucking tailor's dummy, with some insane, serial-killing sociopath kicking your head around a football pitch? The end's the end, but there are certainly more dignified ways to finish up. Being buried whole would be a start.'

'What happened to his innards?'

'I don't fucking know. The point being, you don't fuck with Mexican drugs cartels, which is quite probably what this businessman belonged to, or was at least connected to. Anyway, nothing happened to me that time. Writing a bad review is one thing, but owing money is quite another.'

'It's a lot of debt.'

'It's a leg-breaker, for sure. I need my fucking head examined. All for a stupid bird.'

'A bird?'

'I've been tapping this woman for six months now. She's fucking beautiful, but married.'

'Married?'

'To some rich American guy. He's always going off to the motherland as she puts it, that's Israel to me and you. He's got some business interests there apparently, in olives, or diamonds, or nuclear weapons. I don't what he does and she never says. Anyway, he's got money and he needs it too, because she just loves spending the fucking stuff. We have to eat at all the top restaurants, Michelin-starred joints, then there's the hotels and the spa breaks, and God knows what else. She's wiped me out. But I had to keep seeing her, so I started betting: horses, dogs, online poker, anything. Hence my troubles with this Siberian fellow.'

'If her husband's rich, couldn't she help you out? Pay off this Siberian guy?'

'Jesus Christ, how the fuck is that going to work? She doesn't know about any of this. She thinks I'm some kind of media star that earns a fortune. She's beautiful, she's sexy, she's never done a day's work in her life. I'm a sideline for her: an amusement, her little pet. It's so fucking undignified. If I was half the man I should be, I'd put a pistol to my head and blow my brains out. But I don't have a gun, or the courage to use it. Besides which, if I was dead I wouldn't be able to see her again and I need to keep seeing her. You can understand, can't you? People expect this kind of histrionics from an artist, but not from a journalist. I'm not supposed to go out in a blaze of glory, defiant of history. Do you think she'll care that I'm lying, crucified to my own floorboards? She'll just retire back into the isolation of her money and her dodgy husband, then find herself a new pet to play with.'

'You want me to speak to this Siberian?'

'I want you to pay him off.'

'With what?'

'With money, what else? You've got money. You're rich. Your paintings sell for top prices, have done for a long time. I just wrote you a great review. Haven't you read it yet? I even sent a copy over to your gallery. Anonymously, of course. Look, if you do this for me, I swear I'll pay you back every penny. I'll review every show you put on in the future and give them all a five-star rating. I'll be your greatest champion, just like in the old days, remember.' His voice became higher-pitched, more desperate. 'Jesus Christ, I made you. Those other assholes couldn't see it. They just wanted to write about all that conceptual crap. I'm the only one who could foresee that the future lay in the past. That painting was the future. And you went and fucked all that up.'

'I did.'

'Churning these monotonous pictures out, in a variety of colours. Who cares, as long as there's a market for them. So what if they have no true artistic value anymore. Who cares about experimentation and integrity, so long as your bullshit bourgeois clients are there to pick up the tab.'

'I sold out?' The Painter asked mildly, unoffended.

'Didn't you? Or is it just that you really can't fucking

paint anymore?'

'Can't paint.'

'Look man, help me out, please. Nobody cares about the other stuff, but The Siberian wants his pound of flesh and he's going to take it. I will pay you back, I promise. I've got a meeting set up with a production company to make a two-part television series on the Dadaists. It's a shoe-in and it's good money. Proper professional prime-time shit.' Dan Smithson finished his beer. 'You know what? I can't stand the fucking Dadaists. Help me, please, I'm begging you.'

'Where can I find him?'

'He's got an office in a smart building, working under the dubious cover of financial services. Pretending he's legit. Christ, he probably even pays his fucking taxes.'

The Painter felt in his pockets and pulled out a small silver rectangle.

Smithson leaned over and grabbed it from his hand. 'Let's get the number.' He pushed a button and the screen lit up. He examined the phone curiously. 'Isn't this Hans Zimmer's phone?' Smithson pulled out his own phone and pressed some buttons. 'I'll text over the address so you can go and see him.'

The Painter put down his glass and moved off the bar stool. Dan gripped hold of his left arm. 'I don't want to be crucified, man.'

The Painter stared at the critic's glassy eyes and simply nodded. As they separated, Smithson ordered another beer from the barman.

The street outside the bar was quiet; Sunday night-quiet. It felt cold and unstable. The Painter walked out into the road and watched attentively, waiting for it to rear up and split in half and for the boiling lava to flow freely through the city's labyrinth; choking its alleyways, passageways and pedestrian tributaries. Melting its way through avenues, thoroughfares, grand routes, highways and byways. Suffocating the metropolis into a hell-bound collapse.

The Painter felt exhausted and abandoned beyond repair. He stood beside the Porsche and observed the gleam from the night-time mist on the side of the car. It was damp from the sweat of the city's humming atmosphere. He unzipped his fly and proceeded to piss on the passenger door. He swished his hips from side to side, hoping to cleanse the wretched pollutants. The urine glowed warmth and spun steam into the air as it ran greedily down the smooth metal sheen.

As The Painter adjusted his trousers, he noticed the long, scrawled mark along the side of the car. He placed his fingers along its furrow. There was a minor gouge running down the car's length. Someone had taken a sharpened object and marched along the street scoring the landscape, redressing its imbalance of gloss and shine. The Painter took his keys from his pocket and with them made a parallel mark to the one which already existed. He laughed gently to himself and watched as a tortoiseshell tabby cat ducked inside a doorway across the other side of the street.

A foursome of couples danced merrily down the pavement somewhere behind him. One pair stopped for a minute to kiss tenderly under the orange vacuum of a streetlamp. The young woman's right leg appeared raised slightly, as though fixed in a pose in a magnum photographer's quickly snapped image.

The Painter gripped the roof of the car. He licked a little moisture from its body. It felt cool on his tongue and he rested, leaning on the damp metal surface. He took the key from his pocket and got in. He looked over the interior. It wasn't his car; it was Hans'. The Painter didn't even own a car. Perhaps sometime in the past he had, but not now. Unconcerned, he started the Porsche and headed back to his studio.

The city was lit up like a dirty angel; one with no wings. The buses, taxis, cars and sirens grappled with the nocturnal streets. The traffic lights blinked amber, red and green, with a melancholic nostalgia for pedestrians, gridlock and the renewal of the coming dawn. A time when their fury would jolt with the somnambulistic casualties of the Monday morning commute.

The Painter stuttered and swerved his way home. Temporarily controlling his fatigue before drifting off again towards an apathetic inertia. He passed two police cars on the way. One with lights flashing, the other ambling through the night. He seized control of the wheel and steered pathologically ahead, until out of sight, before returning once more to his slovenly masquerade.

The street across from his building was in full swing now. Vans and lorries leaving and going as quickly as possible. There were stained white coats and hats bobbing around the pavement outside of the market. The Painter looked away and tumbled himself from the car and into the building with as much ease and grace as he could muster.

Once inside the entrance there was quiet and serenity. He breathed heavily as he clambered for the stairs. He stubbornly pulled his own weight against gravity, one step at a time, until he reached the first floor. He bashed his way through the door and on into the dark corridor. His keys eventually found their way into the lock after several abortive attempts.

The studio was passive in its street-lit glow. It felt like a long time since he had left its comfort. He wandered into the living space and managed to make it halfway to the bed before his legs began to buckle under the exertion. He threw himself forward for one final effort and landed face-down, half on the mattress and half on the floor. He dragged himself by his fingers fully onto the bed and, with exhausted relief, passed out.

CHAPTER 9

It was a cold shiver running through his body that finally dragged The Painter into consciousness once more. A sheet lay draped over his torso, while the remains of his naked body withered in the morning chill. His right hand was stuck hard to the undersheet. He peeled the raw flesh slowly and painfully away from its accidental night-time dressing. The Painter groaned wearily as the wound detached itself from the scarred tissue, which remained attached to the smooth white sheet. There was a muddy red bruise left on the crisp, clean space, where once his hand had slept.

He tried to move his head closer to the stain, but couldn't get past the scrap of bedding next to his face, covered as it was in a brownish, orange swirl of vomit.

He forced himself up onto his left elbow and viewed the slick of sickness from a more comforting distance. It had sprayed itself up the sheet and underneath the pillow. Most of the liquid had dried into the cotton weave, but the more visceral lumps were still damp and rancorous.

The Painter edged his nose closer to the vomit. He could smell the extracted contents of alcohol, pulses and stomach bile. He pinched a lump between his forefinger and thumb, then jammed it in his mouth.

It tasted grainy and bitter and was swiftly joined by other particles of vomit, fresh from The Painter's stomach. He retched hard over the pillow, but only a small amount of fluid spat out.

He left the final drools of saliva to tumble inelegantly from his mouth onto his shuddering chest. His staccato panting filled the air, as tears streamed down his cheeks. He finally sat upright and wiped his face with the back of his trembling right hand.

The Painter's whole body convulsed as spasmodic tremors washed over his stomach. He gathered the sheet around his shoulders and held it tightly across his upper body.

Across the room was a large, cast-iron radiator. The Painter shuffled his way over and gripped hold of it. The heavy, painted columns stood cold and dormant. He glanced around the room, looking for a thermostat, but there didn't appear to be one. He considered where he might find a boiler of some sort. The bathroom, perhaps, or the studio?

He held on to the radiator as his legs slid to the floor. The sheet flopped down beside him. He felt the bubbles of cream paint on the iron. He picked at a small crust and revealed a smooth, brown surface underneath. He tried chipping at it with his nails, but they were raw and stiff. He then attempted to gnaw at it with his teeth. All this action produced was an ineffectual chattering of enamel teeth against enamel paint.

The Painter's hand clasped a valve to the left of the radiator. He instinctually turned it clockwise and as he did so the pipes responded with a clatter and clunk.

He pulled the sheet up around himself again and viewed the pile of clothing by the bed. His suit from the day before lay crumpled and dishevelled from its baleful exertions. He examined a purple swelling on his right calf. He poked it with his finger and winced. Then he squeezed hard at the bruised flesh and watched as the blue-and-red stain spread outwards. It was a fresh and painful injury. He looked at the wooden surround of his bed and pondered its culpability.

The Painter leaned his head back and pushed himself up against the hard metal of the radiator. He started to feel the swelling warmth moving up its columns. He felt an increasing heat upon his back, as he closed his eyes against the despairing cling of a new day.

He was wrestled from his solitude by a thud, which came from outside the room, in the corridor. The Painter turned his head towards the door which led through to the bathroom. He spun himself onto his hands and knees, then tried to elevate himself with the use of the radiator. He pulled his left hand away immediately after scalding it on the hot metal. He groaned as he placed the hand back onto the cool parquet flooring.

The Painter placed his nose close to the scuffed floor and smelled the faded varnish and hints of ancient wood. He could see the minute dust particles running along the tight, almost non-existent, grooves, linking in the patterned blocks. He could make out the delicate arabesques of intricate scratches woven into the surface of the wood. He tried scratching some more, but his claws were no match for the material's rigidity. Instead, he attempted to spit out across its surface. His mouth would not respond, except for a few frothing bubbles of saliva escaping onto his chin. Finally, he bundled the sheet around himself and tried to sleep.

The hardness of the floor and the intense heat, now emanating from the radiator, would not allow The Painter any quarter. He wrestled his way free of the sheet, before once more gripping the radiator for support. An intense pain immediately seized the wound in his right hand. He howled in agony as newly-formed blood began to gather at the surface of the skin. The Painter instinctively bound the injured hand with a corner of the bedding, as he soothed himself with regulated breathing.

He crawled free from the heat on all fours, benignly followed by the trailing sheet. He watched as the soft cotton gently brushed itself along the unyielding wood flooring with a lisping swish. He twirled the sheet around and around, flashing white against brown, working its way up into a crazed, whipping motion. The Painter began thrashing the sheet, back and forth across the parquet flooring, watching intently as blocks disappeared and reappeared in the blink of an eye.

Eventually, his arm grew weary of the exertion and he tossed the sheet aside. He stretched his body out fully on the floor and directed his limbs into a star shape. He stared at his hands and feet and pictured them with strong, shining metal nails pinioning them to the wood. He wondered if The Siberian would also crucify Dan Smithson's cock. The ecstasy of power.

He took his nails and scraped them along his chest. They left red traces of their outline on the surface, but refused to properly penetrate the skin. His eyes closed to see different hands. Long talons, primed with crimson nail polish, digging heavy welts into his chest, as luminous green eyes scourged him with contempt. The red of the fingers, the lips, the hair, scorning him with their fearsome ridicule.

He stared over to his left. In the corridor outside the room, lying on the floor, was a magazine. He raised his head slightly in an attempt to see its cover, but his eyesight could not stretch that far. He twisted himself around and onto his side. Looking directly at the spine of the magazine, he could make out the letters A and C only. The Painter used his left index finger to trace the letters, as he mouthed them wordlessly to himself. It was language, the beginnings of the alphabet, of communication. He tried to remember when he had first heard those letters and when he had first used them.

Rolling onto his back once again, he stared up at the ceiling: its blankness. He raised the same finger with which he had traced the words and scrolled them out onto the white painted plaster. He could not reach high enough to make the marks. He spat up at the ceiling instead. Particles of saliva brushed his cheeks and his hair, but their trajectory was incapable of staining the purity of whiteness above.

The Painter heaved himself onto all fours. His stomach was wrenching again and making him groan. He limped over to the magazine in a wounded pose. Once above its cover, he looked down. Taking up the central space was a sculpted ebony face. Part terrifying and part benign, its eyes were diamond-shaped and its teeth small and white. The cheeks were carved sharp and the head was oblong and smooth. It was set within the confines of a glass case in a museum. The coverline stated: 'African Masks: a totem of the 20th Century re-evaluated for the 21st Century'.

The Painter placed his forehead in unison with the forehead of the sculpture on the magazine cover. He rubbed his skin against the glossy, smooth paper. He wanted to imprint the image onto his skull. Stain itself on his blood. He took his right thumb and made a carving motion around his face. Feeling along the bone, into the crevices, over the contours. He pictured himself, in his mind, as a mask. An off-white bone mask, cracked and seeping blood, which was gathering in a pool beneath him. Spreading itself outwards, through the little gaps in the floor and down the walls of the building. A vast avalanche of blood, bathing the streets below him, running through city and countryside, through the sewers and out into the oceans.

He listened to the urine splashing against the floor and swishing underneath his arms and onto the magazine. It smelled stale and warm and it had a rusting, yellow pallor.

The Painter dipped his nose down into the puddle of piss and blew bubbles through his nostrils. Droplets of urine splashed against his mouth and chin. He lifted his head and looked down his body, towards his penis, to witness the last drip fall from his foreskin onto the wood floor. A mild shudder ran up his body as a chill passed through him.

The smell of urine in his nostrils and the taste of vomit on his tongue gave The Painter a feverish momentum. He rushed from the spot, crashing into the bathroom and gagging over the sink. His stomach went into a form of spasmic revulsion, but there was no sickness forthcoming. Tears bathed his cheeks as he viewed a few spots of blood staining the white porcelain sink. The Painter began picking at them in an attempt to erase them. He turned the red tap on and waited as the warm water swished around the sink. The blood drops stubbornly rinsed through, turning pinkish as they swirled down the plughole.

The Painter cupped a handful of steaming water running from the tap and hurled it at himself. The pain was immediate and intense, it stung his entire face and parts of his chest. He howled in a reflex of abandon at the excruciating force of the heat. The impacted skin burned raw with a scalding inflammation. He ricocheted off the bathroom wall, to beneath the shower, which he threw on in the full blue position. The shock of the freezing water was no less devastating for his body. He shook violently and cried out piteously as the shower drove a hard spray of water over his battered, naked body.

He swung out his right fist and punched a tile on the wall, splitting his knuckle open on the grout. A blossoming of blood ran down the gap in the tiles. The Painter watched as a red streak formed down the wall. He placed his fist in the next gap along and let the blood run vertically down that shallow well too. The streams of blood formed a symmetrical pattern on the wall: white, followed by red, followed by white, followed by red, followed by white.

The Painter began to shiver uncontrollably. His skin tight and pinched, his body battered and weary, raw and weeping. He turned the shower off and glanced up at the shining silver dome, shot through with dozens of pin-prick holes, which dribbled their last gasps of invigoration.

Stumbling dazed and cleansed from the shower, The Painter gripped hold of a warm, white cotton towel from a hot metal rail. He pushed his face into it and breathed heavily through its soft fibres. As he pulled his face away again, he noticed the subtle indentation he had left in the towel's fabric. He pictured his skeletal mask, all bone and blood, white and red.

The Painter began to gently dab his wounded frame with the towel and felt a rictus of warmth pass down his body. He secured the towel around his waist and wandered back into the hallway outside the bathroom.

He stared at the door, through which the magazine had been delivered. He wondered if he had noticed the door when he had visited the night before. Had it been there all this time?

The Painter placed his hand in the rectangular cut-out in the wood of the door, for the letterbox. It was a crude hole, rough-edged. The Painter scraped his cut knuckle against it and began sawing backwards and forwards. The raw graze widened slightly in the ensuing motion. He finally pulled his hand away and viewed the tissue damage. He examined the wound to see if the injury had reached the white of the bone, then he examined the door to see if he had left splintered fragments of bone embedded in the wood. There were none.

Disappointed, The Painter turned his attention to a lock in the door. He moved his hand up and turned it anti-clockwise. He pulled the door inwards and glanced outside. It was the same corridor which held the entrance to the studio. He stared out towards the stairway, but nobody stirred. It was as dark and quiet as always.

He closed the door again and pushed his head against it. Looking down, he noticed the magazine sitting on the floor. *Art and Culture*. Wasn't that the magazine that Dan Smithson had mentioned the previous night; the one which Emily had referred to in her message? Was there an article regarding an exhibition of his work?

The Painter bent down and picked up the magazine. He walked through to the living space and over to the sofa. Still in his towel, he sat on the cool, soft leather and placed his hand on the cold, chrome bars running around the outside. He gripped one bar tightly and held it for a moment. He tried pulling it hard, away from the rest of the furnishing, but it wouldn't budge.

The Painter stared again at the detached face of the African mask. It felt both real and inanimate; a benign object filled with malevolent spirits, or a malevolent object filled with benign spirits. He wished to sketch it, give it weight and depth on the page, animate it and give it rebirth into the world. Set it free to reign as it saw fit. Place darkness and light on a blank white sheet and reinterpret an artefact as an ambiguity of space and meaning.

The Painter held the page up to his face and screamed dementedly at it. He held the magazine to his ear and flicked through the pages. They moved through his fingers in a crisp and efficient manner. The wisps of air they generated tickled his ear.

He held the magazine up to his nose and fanned the pages before it. They had the aroma of a fresh and vibrant chemical dye, lovingly pasted over the finest pulped and processed trees. This was complimented by a nervous and dynamic energy. The spine felt solid and noble, self-assured and authoritative. The Painter began to tentatively scan the insides of the magazine.

There was a retrospective for an artist named Keith Haring, filled with stripy designs and a man in glasses blending in with his environment. There was an advertisement for Louis Vuitton luggage. On another page, notice of an up-and-coming art auction in New York. Pictured on the page was a sculpture by Constantin Brâncusi of a bird in flight, rendered in a highly abstracted manner. There was an antiquities symposium being held in Athens, an art fair in Switzerland, and various universities were advertising MA programmes in Fine Art, History of Art, Curatorship, Film, Photography, Design, and Creative Writing.

An exhibition was titled *The Past Future Explained: a complete survey of Archigram Projects*. This title was set over a drawing representing an elongated blob with some holes cut into it and various scatological marks. An art institution in the Far East was holding an exhibition linking the artistic practices of Picasso and Matisse. On the left side of the page was an image of Picasso in a black martial arts uniform, performing a high kick with his right foot. On the right side of the page, Matisse posed in a red martial arts uniform, blocking the kick with his left arm. Above this montage was placed a simple reference: 'Picasso v Matisse'. The name Picasso was in blue, Matisse in yellow.

There were pages of advertisements for Italian and Scandinavian furniture, chic leather handbags, tailored English suits, and airline companies which ferried people to and from the most exotic locations in the world. There was a big, four-tiered ring from Boucheron and a blue-bottled aftershave by Chanel.

A European institution was opening a foreign branch, designed by a Japanese architect, somewhere in the Middle East. The desert was to be filled with Renaissance paintings.

Towards the middle of the magazine there was also a three-page spread analysing a recent production of Igor Stravinsky's *The Rite of Spring* in Berlin. There was a re-examination of the legacy of Kurt Schwitters, an homage to the films of Jean Cocteau, and one to London Soho's bohemian life in the 1950s. There was an article lamenting the passage of *Life* magazine and its contribution to the world of photography.

Then The Painter came across the article. A four-page spread entitled *Immanence Transcendence Permanence: a primer for the future of painting, by Dan Smithson*.

The Painter looked at the accompanying images. There were six paintings and a white gallery space where still more were hung on the walls. He scanned the paintings. They were at once familiar and yet remote, as though created with someone else's hands. He recognised them, but were they paintings that he had created?

He began to read the piece, skimming through various parts. 'These paintings are there to remind us of the montage of imagery passing through our minds in the spaces in between our acting consciousness. They speak as much of sensations, palettes, feelings and those clinging memories, that haunt us, but which are, nevertheless, beyond our active reach… The orange streaks appear to float above the richer, deeper reds… The surface ripples and shimmers with tension… The eye darts around in maniacal response to the enveloping glut of the depth of strokes, squiggles, slashes and scatterings of paint… The paint, in places thickened, in others thinned out… The canvases appear both glued hard to the walls yet floating in the ethereal space surrounding them… It is the newness and verve of the digitised world and the greatly redefined space of the gallery construct, which has given painting a rebirth and a contemporaneousness which it struggled to endure in the dying stages of the 20th Century. The globalised world and the new century will not be restricted or bound by any rules or laws. It is an ill-defined, amorphous future we contemplate. All certainties have evaporated; all bets are off… If everything can be art what may we value?... Painting has reached its perfect juncture: all pictorial space is permissible.'

Smithson had signed the piece off with a declaration. 'The images here have as fast a flow of information and hyper-connectivity as any internet plug-in. The pieces presented here are desperately modern, but they also have a long and distinguished lineage, not something every work of art in the contemporary gallery space can claim.'

The magazine slipped from The Painter's fingers and dropped onto the floor. He hadn't understood a word of it.

The images felt real and imaginary, as though he had at some time simply dreamt them and here they had appeared in print. They were detached mirages squinting out from the paper.

He took the magazine once more and began tearing at its pages. Ripping them apart with his teeth before spitting them out again. He took the discarded, soggy tracts and pushed them up into his arse. He squeezed them in and then clenched his cheeks hard, before trying to push them free again with his sphincter muscles. They remained in situ and so instead be began to bounce up and down on the sofa. The hard edges of the paper cut and stabbed at his skin. When he finally pulled them out by hand they were soiled with traces of saliva, excrement, and blood.

The Painter sniffed at a piece and recoiled. The scent was a vapid trace of bodily expungement: a minor whiff of death. True decay felt dusty and powdery, the rotting corpse having long abandoned the bones. The immediate act of death itself was filled with biological and chemical discharge.

He sat down on the sofa and clawed at his naked form. He scratched welts into his shoulder blades. He punched his nose hard until his eyes watered and his nostrils bled. He took the mangled pieces of print from the floor and wiped his tears and blood away with them. The magazine copy was crumpled and abrasive on his skin. He cursed himself through his fingers and looked tenderly at the now disfigured image of the beautiful African mask on the front page.

The Painter's hands trembled as he sifted through the paper debris to find the article by Dan Smithson. It was torn and deformed, the words an even further esoteric collage of half-sentences and opaque reasoning.

The Painter bundled the magazine together in his hands and stumbled over towards the place on the floor where urine still sat fermenting. He ripped at the magazine pages and flung them onto the piss, soaking up the liquid into the glossy print. The pages of the magazine darkened as they drank up the putrid fluid. He stamped on them furiously and used the sole of his foot to swirl them about the floor.

The one name, which seemed to stand out from the mulched copy and had impregnated a negative of itself onto the skin of The Painter's foot, was Dan Smithson.

He remembered his promise to visit The Siberian: a bookmaker, debt collector, financial advisor and sadistic psychopath. The Painter wondered if he might survive such a meeting. Would The Siberian roar up from his chair, leap over his desk, brandishing a gleaming, open-cut razor, and slit The Painter's throat open, then lay his tongue on The Painter's clavicle to collect the blood?

The Painter closed his eyes and pictured his blood pouring out from the infectious wound, encrusted with flakes of brown, papery skin and yellow, jaundiced pus, staining the warm, bubbling river of a sweet and radiant red, which felt tantalisingly unctuous in his mouth, pouring down his throat and into his gut, to be boiled in acid. His stomach lurched into paralysis, momentarily holding a spasm. It finally recoiled into submission and for the first time that day, The Painter thought about food.

There had to be some form of eatery close by: a café, a deli, or a bar, where he could get a cup of coffee, a sandwich, or a pastry.

The Painter hauled himself up from the sofa and made his way cautiously towards the locker and filing cabinet that held his clothes. He pulled on one of the metal drawers and took out a black, v-necked, cotton t-shirt. He smelled its cool, clean freshness and smoothed it around his face, before lugubriously pulling it over his head. His arms felt little equal to the task, but he continued to dress in spite of his ailing fatigue. He put on black cotton shorts and black cotton socks. His limbs ached from the exertion.

The Painter closed his eyes and reached out for the

comfort and relief of sleep. It felt dark and dense in his head, as though the inside of his mind might implode and fold into itself at any given moment. He staggered backwards and hit his hand against a bookshelf. It was sufficient to refocus and re-orientate him.

He moved over to the metal locker to retrieve a black woollen suit. It felt more abrasive and of inferior quality to the one he had worn the day before, but the trousers fitted perfectly and the jacket was tailored in to his waist and sat squarely on his shoulders.

'This is mine. This is meant for me,' he stated quietly to himself.

He began to rub his palms down the trousers and along his chest. The clothing built an armoury against his nakedness. He could no longer feel his form; his perfect outline. He took his right index finger and gently ran it down his left arm and up under his armpit. He pressed his finger into the joint at his elbow and felt along the crease. He lifted his left arm up and felt underneath his shoulder blade; he moved it up and down in his hand.

The Painter walked to the corridor and then into the bathroom. He looked in the mirror at the reflection of an oblique face he half-recognised. Had he ever drawn that face? It would be better to film it. The mechanical eye staring unwaveringly at the biological eye. Both captured in a stalemate. Which would flinch first?

He slowly closed his right eye and then slowly opened it again. He repeated this action several times. The Painter then tried opening and closing his right eye in rapid succession at twenty-four times per second. He was unable to perform the task adequately. His reflection began to exhibit a sense of flotation and movement.

The image flickered and resisted absolute resolution of accuracy. In between blinks the image disappeared; it simply ceased to exist.

The Painter closed his eyes in an attempt to capture the

radiance of darkness. The lack of an image comforted him and he rested his head against the cool of the mirror. He pursed his lips and silently pressed them against their reflective negative image. He pictured the other side of the reflection in monochrome. His drawn, pale pink lips a deep grey on a reverse image.

As he lifted his skull away from the mirror he kept his left eye resolutely closed. He panned his head to the right, past the mirror, along the whitewashed wall and on past the small window. He turned his full body rightwards and continued to pan along the white tiles of the shower and the showerhead and on to the white door, where a white terry-towelling dressing gown hung upon a hook.

He hadn't noticed the dressing gown hanging there. Had it always been there? The Painter moved cautiously towards it. He touched it with his hand; he felt it across his face; he caressed it and smelled it. The dressing gown possessed a mildly perfumed scent, which he found soothing. It smelled of someone familiar. It smelled of him.

He searched the bathroom for the source of the aroma. He walked over to a small cabinet hanging on the wall. Inside, there was a blue glass bottle. He pulled the top from the bottle and smelled it. The scent was the same as that of the dressing gown: sickly and bitter. He sprayed the aftershave into his face, towards his nostrils. The burning in his eyes, nose and throat was instantaneous. He dropped the bottle immediately into the sink and screamed out in agony.

The Painter struggled to catch his breath as the bottle smashed into several large chunks of glass. The smell of the aftershave burst violently into the air. He gasped in its fumes and, in trying to escape, walked into the wall of the shower.

Eventually gripping his way along the wall and out of the room, The Painter stumbled into the living space. His eyes began to water. The salt and alcohol began running into his mouth. Through blurred vision, he located a sheet from the bed and, gripping hold of it tightly, raised it to his face. He wiped aggressively at the tears now streaming from his eyes. The cotton cloth pressed in tight made the pain more excruciating. He could not lift the sheet from his face. He stood breathing hard into its tightly-woven gauze. His head began to lighten and pins and needles passed down his legs and into his feet. The Painter gripped the sheet tighter still around his face, until he could hardly breathe at all. The anaesthetising smell of the aftershave gradually faded, as did the semi-luminous white through the sheet.

It was the high-pitched throbbing in his head which he first felt. The fingers of his right hand crawled gravely along the wooden parquet. The air he breathed through his nose gurgled thickly on the floor. His mouth felt dry and raw, with the tingling sensation of perfumed metal.

The Painter opened his eyes to an intense and thick white. It was a blinding radiance which was both uniform and all-pervasive. He blinked open and closed his fever-saturated eyes; the sight remained dim. He then crunched open and closed the toes on his right foot, and those of his left. His reflexes were slow but his joints responded. He was neither dead nor paralysed.

Next came his hands. He pushed both palms close to his body and with an intensive focus managed to raise himself off the floor. The sheet which had covered his head fell away, leaving The Painter with an imperfect vision of the room. His only concern then was to traverse the narrow space to the bed in as few steps as possible. He made it far enough to throw his torso on the mattress and his head on a pillow.

The lights flashed and spat around the inner sanctum of his skull. The Painter's breathing was dry and laboured. His body had supplanted itself into a position of levitation.

There was no longer a mattress, a pillow, or sheets beneath him. There was only an expanse of air flowing around his atrophied state. There were no sounds or smells and nothing left to feel. His vision was impaired inwards. All that surrounded him was a place filled with a kind of nocturnal death.

Somewhere in the space deep below him came a repetitive trilling. The Painter's mind grappled towards it. Willing it up into his consciousness. It drew closer and louder, then discontinued completely. His voice echoed within its hollow carapace. The expressions and words disjointed and cavernous. He attempted to mouth them: repeat their trajectory. His body began twisting in a slowly submerging tunnel. The words became sharper and more resonant. 'Can you hear me? Are you okay?' They were no longer an inner voice, his voice, but someone else's. It was a soothing voice. A female voice. 'Are you okay? Can you speak? Can you hear me?'

The Painter's eyes limply opened to reveal the face of a young woman. She sat above him on the bed, with a concerned expression on her face. He looked straight into her large, green, baby-doll eyes, dripping thick with black mascara. Her skin was a peerless white and her small, full lips a shining crimson. When she opened her mouth to ask him once again if he was okay, her teeth sparkled a Californian white. The Painter stared up at her glossy red hair, bobbed to meet her sharp, delicate jawline.

She was an apparition: an invention of his subconscious. He was asleep or unconscious or perhaps even dead. This woman wasn't real, he had imagined her. She had visited him already, but she was different then, stylised and idealised in his imagination. The Painter wondered who it was he dreamed of; it wasn't this woman, not entirely. The lynx-eyed beauty was someone else. He knew the beauty before him: it was Emily.

'Do you want some water?' she asked.

Standing up, Emily showed off a tall, slender figure in a black mid-length wool coat with a cowl neckline. She wore a pair of shimmering black tights and her calves were accentuated by a pair of black, high-heeled laced-up ankle boots. Around her neck was a thin piece of black silk knotted in a pussy bow at the front. Emily's walk was as elegant and effortless as her accent.

As she went towards the kitchen, she stopped in front of the sofa and picked up the copy of *Art and Culture*. She held the corner cautiously between the finger and thumb of her black satin gloves. She raised the magazine up to her nose and sniffed at it without emotion. She turned to The Painter and stated coldly, 'I see you've read the copy of the magazine I had sent round.'

Emily placed the journal ceremoniously on the coffee table. She looked at her fingers then sniffed at them, before scouring the room with her eyes. 'I should have brought latex gloves and a bin bag. This place looks like a fucking crime scene.' Her expression became suddenly weary. 'Is this paint or blood I'm seeing everywhere?' She lifted the heel of her shoe and looked at the unidentified debris she had collected on the soles. 'I knew I should have worn an old pair. Bastard artists.' She looked at the walls. 'Is this the career I've really chosen? All this to have my own gallery.'

'Why are you here?' The Painter grumbled.

'Francesca sent me to accompany you to this evening's opening for Samantha Kilgore's new show at the gallery. She wants all her little artists present, as a show of solidarity. It's a three-line whip and I'm here to make sure you're on message.'

'On message?'

'You're not to fuck up,' Emily explained, exasperated. 'That little weasel Dan Smithson's written you up a good piece in *Art and Culture*. God knows why. He must be after something. You're to give a good soundbite, lots of praise and all that. Don't swear, don't drool, don't slur, and definitely don't bleed. Chew food only with your mouth closed and sound sophisticated and erudite. You can do erudite, can't you? You can be a clever little shit when you want to. I've heard you.' Emily picked up a cup and sniffed its inside.

'What time is it?' stumbled The Painter.

'Five o'clock. I've come early. I knew you'd be in a state.' She surveyed him, critically assessing him. 'Get in a fight again? Who with this time? Another painter, a critic, a girlfriend, the husband of a girlfriend? All of the above? You're a bad boy, aren't you? Born to play the role. And you do it so effortlessly.'

'I had an accident.'

'Fell down some stairs, did you, and landed up your own arse?'

'My own arse?'

'Being coy. It's not like you.'

'I hurt everywhere.'

'No doubt in your kidneys, liver and veins more than anywhere.'

'It feels cyclical. A moveable feast.'

She tapped her foot impatiently. 'I admired you. Do you know that?'

'Admired me?'

'When I was at art school. I remember going to your exhibition and crying when I left.' Emily filled the cup she was holding with water.

'Why did you cry?'

'I thought your paintings were so beautiful and ugly and strange and liberating and I knew then that my artistic career was over.'

'Over?'

'Before it even got started. I realised that no matter how good I could get, it would never be that good. I was a painter then. After which I tried sculpture, photography, film, performance. I sang in a band for a time. We had one minor single. But what I really wanted to do was paint.' Emily took the cup of water over to The Painter and sat down beside him once more on the bed. She lifted his head and gave him a sip. 'I saw you in a bar once. I wanted to come over and chat to you, but you were with a girl, some supermodel type, and she was all over you. There was a group of people surrounding you like an art entourage. You were pissed and holding forth on how insincere Picasso was. That he was no more interested in Guernica than he was in white doves and communism. That the only thing Picasso was interested in was Picasso. You called him a talented shit.'

'Picasso. Pi. Ca. So.' The Painter mouthed the sounds.

'There's always someone else: someone better; someone smarter; someone newer, shinier, more talented. I'll have to find my own.'

'Your own what?'

'My own version of you. A golden goose.'

'Is that how you view me?'

'That's how Francesca views you. That's why your presence is requested at the gallery tonight. That's why she sent me.'

'You?'

'She's no fool. She knows you well enough. "Wear something sexy," she told me. "That should pique his interest." You're a star. She needs you there. The collectors all love you. It authenticates her latest acquisition.'

'Her falling star.'

'Don't be so sure. Your prices are holding up remarkably well.' Emily was every bit the aspiring gallerist. 'In fact, they're on the rise. I sold one today. Very derivative, but princely priced. I owe you for a sweet commission. So I thought I'd be nice to you and dress the part. A classy kind of slut. Just like you always order.'

'I don't pay for it.'

'Don't you? We all pay one way or another. Everything's a transaction. You see, I've learned the business well.'

Emily stood up and unbuttoned her coat, walked over to the sofa, and carefully placed it on an unsullied arm. She wore a short black leather dress, cut off at the shoulders, a zip running all the way up the front, culminating at the neck with a round fastener. A white stripe followed the zip all the way up. Her black gloves carried along her forearm to her elbows. The Painter stared at her, mesmerised. She could have swaggered up any catwalk in the world. She could have sold old sack cloth to a silk merchant.

Emily turned towards him and narrowed her emerald eyes to a freeze-frame of hatred. There was the look. It had been her all along. He wanted her to stay with him for eternity. He could lie there in a state of glorious death and she could swarm around him and talk and be beautiful. She would never grow old and his presence would never become a bore.

'God, you've grown ugly. You used to be handsome. I could have slept with you back then.'

'Back when?'

'Eight or nine years ago. When I was a student. I kept a picture of you on the wall of my studio space. You were wearing a slim, grey suit and nothing else. No shirt or tie. No shoes or socks. Just you in a suit, holding an open black umbrella above your head, sitting on a Marcel Breuer chair in Francesca's old gallery, surrounded by your paintings, gleaming on the walls. It was a sell-out show. The biggest of the season. You were a star. All the boys on my course wanted to be you and all the girls wanted to sleep with you. Well, that's what we told ourselves. That's what we always tell ourselves.'

'Why are you telling me this?'

'I was in love with a boy. I stopped painting and I broke his heart.'

'Because of me?'

'You're still vain, though,' her eyes coolly assessed him. 'No, not because of you, because of me. I stopped painting and I stopped loving him. He died in a car accident six months later. He was full of alcohol and drugs. I went to the mortuary to try and see his body, but they wouldn't let me see it. I made a terrible scene. I wanted to touch him and feel his wounds. I wanted to make him alive again. I wanted to love him again. But he was gone. Then he was cremated and turned into ash. His mother called me a whore at the funeral. So I went back and slept with his best friend. Then his girlfriend called me a whore as well. I never thought I would survive it all back then. I even stole my mother's sleeping pills once. But I just got drunk instead and fucked one of my lecturers. I miss him still.'

'Who?'

'The boy with the broken heart. The only boy I've ever loved. And I gave him up because of your paintings. Because I wanted to be you and he couldn't understand why.'

'He was a painter?'

'He was an architecture student. He thought you were overrated.'

'I am.'

'He didn't know art. Not the way you do. Not the way I did.'

'He died because of art.'

'He died because I broke his heart. He died because I could no longer paint and because I couldn't conceive of a world where I couldn't paint. He died because I loved him and I couldn't bear to look at him anymore. The same way I couldn't bear to look at a canvas anymore. And now I stare at them all the time and I sell them. I'll get a nice fat cheque because of your painting and he'll still be dead and

I'll still love him.'

'I don't remember that show.'

'I'm surprised you can remember anything. All that partying, boozing, drugging and whoring around. What can you remember of exhibitions or art? What does any of it matter, anyway? They're still willing to pay huge sums of money for your canvases. Your provenance is secure. Maybe they all think you're going to die soon. But we both know better, don't we? Your type seldom die.'

'You don't like me much.'

'I don't have to like you much. That's not what I'm paid for. That's not what I'm here for.'

'How did you get in?'

'I rang the bell, but you didn't answer so I used the key to your studio that Francesca gave me.'

'Francesca has a key to my studio.' It was a statement. The real question was: who was Francesca?

'Of course she does. How the hell else would we get a hold of your paintings? You're never done with the damn things so we have to send round a couple of gorillas with white gloves and a truck to take them.'

'They aren't finished.'

'They're never finished. That's the problem with geniuses, they're never through having to prove to us all what geniuses they are. Don't take it too personally, it's just economics.'

'Can I have my key back?'

'No, it's Francesca's key. She'll fire me.'

'I don't want her to have it.'

'Relax. Perhaps she needs it for another reason. Some secret sexual rendezvous in the night. You might get lucky. You certainly wouldn't be the first.'

The Painter raised himself up in the bed. He held out his hand towards the long, thin, black leather clutch bag placed on the bed earlier by Emily. He ran his finger along the soft and smooth surface. He picked it up and smelled it. There was still a faint tang of animal hide held within its pores. There was a small, silver metal clasp. The Painter bit softly into it.

'The key's not in the bag. It's in my coat pocket,' Emily remarked nonchalantly. 'I didn't think bags would be your kind of thing.'

The Painter rubbed the piece of leather against his face. Then he rubbed it against the back of his hand.

Emily watched him with mounting curiosity. 'Be careful, that's designer.' But her comment was lacklustre. She was fascinated by The Painter's actions.

He bit into the bag then licked along its skin. He imagined Emily's leg. The static of the tights running through his tongue. Electricity creased through his body, stimulating all his nerve endings as he looked towards her. But Emily had gone. She was caressing the open wounds of the boy she loved, lying on a slab in the mortuary. The skin grey and cold. The eyes glassed and dull. The alcohol and drugs evaporated. Emily could feel the dead body. The dry wounds. The cut skin. The cold blubber. Closing the lids down on eyes that would never see this world again. Their focus and all the images they had looked upon gone forever. Emily would lie down with him on the metal tray, under the harsh fluorescent bulbs, within that emotionless expanse of death. She could hold that boy's disjointed dead hand and offer him forgiveness, tenderness and love.

Emily was standing above The Painter. Her face was pained, her eyes staining red and lurching fast-forward to tears.

'What age was he?' The Painter asked, looking up.

'Twenty.' Emily croaked.

'Twenty.' The Painter swirled the words around in his head as he passed Emily her bag.

She took it and held it to her chest. Her face was basked in horror as the tears began to stream down her cheeks. She sat down delicately on the edge of the bed and pressed the bag against her eyes. Her shoulders shuddered tremulously. Then she too smelled the bag, before wiping the tears collected on its surface all over her face.

'He bought me it.' She spoke quietly.

'The bag?'

'All those years ago now. He bought it for our second anniversary. I saw it in a shop window, but couldn't afford it. So he bought it for me. He bankrupted himself for it, for me. I haven't used it since I ended the relationship.' She stood up and paced around the room for a moment, apparently lost and confused. 'I've felt so strange all day. Ever since I sold that painting of yours.' She opened the bag and looked inside. 'I need to go and sort myself out. I've got to get you ready for this preview opening.' Emily stumbled towards the bathroom.

The Painter remained on the bed, staring up at the ceiling and a long hairline fracture in the white painted plaster. He held an imaginary implement in his right hand and traced the fracture's journey. He then traced the same trajectory in the air in front of his face. His hand movement was frail and quavering. He studied his hand. It had aged dramatically from when he last remembered investigating it. The hand had been the means of his living and of life itself. He rarely looked at it, and never protected it. His hands and eyes had learned total co-dependence on one another. He rarely looked into his eyes, either. His sight had always been good. His hands steady. Now they were fading. He didn't feel he could sketch Emily, as beautiful as she was. In his youth it would have been second nature. As simple and natural as breathing. He would have drawn her, painted her, photographed her and pinned the photos up on the studio wall. When he was too exhausted from the work, he would have taken her out to a restaurant and then taken her home to bed. How many Emilys had he known? Too many. He couldn't remember the women anymore. He couldn't remember the work.

'You are the fruit of your loins.'

The Painter propped himself up on his left elbow. He felt the blood drain from his head down to his torso. He tried to remember what it was he had to do. Was it really five o'clock? Where had time gone? When did he see Dan Smithson? In a bar on Sunday night. Was it Monday? Was it Tuesday? How long had he slept?

Emily walked back into the room. She looked polished and efficient. All traces of her trauma had disappeared: painted over. She stared at The Painter. 'What the hell happened in the bathroom?' Her demeanour was half confusion and half humour.

'Another accident.'

'Christ. It stinks of aftershave. I ran some water through the sink, but I wasn't sticking my hands in there with all that broken glass. Be careful. You'll have a nasty accident with that.' Emily observed him more closely. 'If you haven't already.'

She moved across the room to her coat and put it on. She turned to The Painter. 'Was it an accident?'

'What?'

'The broken aftershave bottle.'

'It fell in the sink when I sprayed it in my eyes.'

Emily laughed. 'My god. What possessed you to spray aftershave in your eyes?'

'I felt compelled to do it.'

'Well, I wouldn't do it a second time.' She gathered herself together and walked over to the bed. 'Time to go, sleepyhead.'

The Painter closed his eyes and lay back down again. Emily swiftly grabbed his right hand, pulling him up and clean off the bed. He steadied himself against her and met her eyes. There was the black pupil, the green iris, and tiny streaks of red veins spanning out from it. Up close, Emily's veneer had slipped a little. She suddenly looked vulnerable. The eyes had a benevolence to them he hadn't noticed from a distance. He wanted to put his mouth up to her eye then suck the ball clean from the socket. He would ingest it and then run his tongue around the damp, blood-drenched cavity.

Emily's eyes narrowed as though she could read his thoughts and she let him go. He stumbled backwards and slumped down on the bed again.

Emily stood above him, her black satin gloves reaching for his neck, her knees pinioning him to the mattress, her thumbs pushing hard against the Adam's apple. The Painter's face contorted, the skin wilting and peeling back, the blood pouring, coagulating, falling and smashing onto the floor, the skull grey with large, bulging, grotesque eyes and bloated, black tongue. Emily licked the craggy, scalped bone all over, with a sickening triumph.

'You need a shave. Are you capable?' Emily looked quizzically at The Painter. He reflected her expression. She turned and walked towards the bathroom.

The Painter gripped hold of the edge of the mattress and trembled slightly. He pinched the undersheet between forefinger and thumb, then rubbed it backwards and forwards in his hand. The soothing motion comforted him and the minor palpitations began to recede.

Emily walked purposefully through from the bathroom. In her hands she carried a can of shaving foam and a straight razor. She placed both items on the bed before marching to the kitchen area. She opened and closed a couple of cupboards until she found what she was looking for. Emily pulled out a large glass Pyrex jug and began filling it with hot water from the sink. She carefully walked over to The Painter, balancing the jug in her right hand. She then placed the jug gently on the floor before kneeling in front of him.

Emily wrapped a sheet around The Painter's shoulders. 'Splash some hot water on your face,' she commanded him coldly.

The Painter dipped his hands in the jug. They immediately stung and he wrenched them from it. He watched the wisps of steam float up to Emily's face. She stared at him passively. He forced his hand in again and cupped a handful of scorching water then threw it at his chin. He grimaced and sucked in his breath as the water enflamed his skin. Emily took the can of shaving foam and shook it vigorously. She captured The Painter's right hand and sprayed a spiral gloop into his palm.

'Put it on your face.' She indicated towards his stubble.

The Painter roughly smeared the white soapy foam all around his jaw, chin and neck. Emily took hold of the bone handle of the razor with her right hand and with her left opened the Sheffield steel blade to a 180-degree angle. She took the left thumb of The Painter and ran the blade delicately across it. The razor nicked his skin mildly and a hint of red spread to the surface. Neither The Painter nor Emily flinched. He looked at her face as she stared at his neck.

She made the first stroke of the blade down his right cheek from the ear. It was a smooth, choreographed move which ended with Emily whipping the razor away as it reached The Painter's jawline. She dipped the razor blade in the water and swished it around rapidly until the foam diluted into the water, turning both a murky, cream colour. Emily continued shaving The Painter's cheeks, chin and upper lip. She held The Painter's nose, pulled it abruptly upwards, and began to shave his neck. The razor floated across the tough skin as she reached his jaw and flipped it away from him.

The Painter felt the blade flaking all the scales of dead skin from his throat. Rinsing them in the absorbent waters of the jug. Purifying his flesh against dermatological disease. She could scrub bleach over the abrasive skin to cleanse the pores further. Washing out each tiny pockmark with an acidic rigour.

Emily finished shaving him. She let go of his nose and washed the razor one final time in the hair-flecked, muddy white water. She cleaned the blade smooth against the sheet and closed it resolutely shut. She then took hold of the sheet and roughly wiped The Painter's face free of all remnants of shaving foam. A trickle of blood deposited itself on the sheet. There was a small cut on the left side of his neck.

Emily looked at the soiled red mark. 'Sorry, I didn't mean to be rough, but I'm not used to doing this sort of thing. I haven't shaved anyone in a long time.'

She stood up and returned the razor blade and can of shaving foam to the bathroom. When she returned she took the glass jug to the kitchen sink and decanted the debris in the bowl, before swirling it clean with hot running water.

The Painter looked confusedly to Emily. 'Where am I going?' he asked in a puzzled voice.

'To the gallery,' Emily replied.

'What gallery?'

'Your gallery. Francesca's gallery.'

'But what for?'

'To attend an opening for one of Francesca's latest artists,' she reminded him patiently.

'I don't like artists.'

Emily smiled to herself. 'Neither do I.'

She walked over to the bed and stood above The Painter. 'You're going to the show.' Her words were weary but uncompromising. She searched around the space until she came across some black leather slip-on shoes. She threw them down at The Painter's feet. 'Put these on.'

The Painter looked at them.

'I've already shaved you. I'm not putting your fucking shoes on for you, too. I'm not your housekeeper or your little slave girl, or whatever servant it is you're used to. I'm doing this under duress as it is.'

'Under duress.' The Painter rolled the words around in his mouth.

Emily smiled sarcastically at him. 'Well, I want to get on, don't I?' She stared at his exhausted eyes. 'Come on, let's get going or we'll be late.'

The Painter took the shoes in his hand. They felt cold but pliable. The soft leather slipped over his feet in a perfect, fluid motion. He curled his toes upwards and gently flexed the material into a few tepid creaks.

Emily walked over to the sofa and retrieved her coat. She buttoned herself into it snugly before collecting her bag from the bed. 'Right, let's go,' she announced as she made her way through the living space to the studio, picking her way around the mess.

The Painter recklessly bobbed through the living area and into the studio. His hands shook slightly and his pulse boomed behind his right eyeball. He looked at the blank canvases and felt the swelling behind his eye reach a crescendo and burst forth, pouring its liquid mucous over the stretched white cotton. The blood-soaked placenta crawled its way downwards one globule at a time. The phlegm-like substance would spread its cool moisture across the canvases.

Emily stood by the door and stretched out her hand. She clicked her fingers twice. 'Come on, genius. Time to go.' She glanced around the studio. 'There's nothing to look at, anyway.' The Painter scanned the large room, the blank canvases, then followed her through the door.

Emily moved swiftly down the staircase. The Painter pursued her with bleary vision, clinging on to the banister with both hands. The smooth wood warmed his palms as his fingers gathered to grip the sides.

Waiting by the open main door, Emily stood translucent in the evening light. Sparkles of dying sunshine illuminated her silhouette. The Painter glanced at the vague mirage of the human form captured in the ethereal light. He missed the last step and came down on the ground on his left knee. He yelped and looked past Emily to the sight of the growing mass of white vans circling the meat-market across the road. The sun hit his eyes as he watched Emily apparently smiling.

She walked over to him and took his left hand. 'If you're going to propose to me, you could pick a more romantic place.'

The Painter raised himself onto his right leg, lifting the left in unison. He staggered a little before gripping hold of the injured leg and willing it onwards. It dragged limply and without enthusiasm into the street.

There was a musky, cool breeze spreading its way down the road. The Painter's newly shaved face tingled with a pert frisson of pain. He moved towards the Porsche, still parked by the side of the road.

Emily was wandering down the street towards a taxi. She turned to see The Painter trying to open the door of the car. She held her place for a moment before approaching him and glancing around the street to see if anyone was watching. 'Are you trying to impress me?' she asked.

'Impress you?'

'By stealing this car.'

'I'm not stealing it.'

Emily surveyed the car by rubbing her hand along its roof. She smiled slyly and moved around to the windscreen. She ripped off the little black-and-yellow striped plastic bag from the windscreen. The Painter looked up to find her dangling it in front of his nose. He took the packet and tossed it into the gutter.

'You are a bad boy, aren't you? They still know whose car it is. You'll still have to pay,' she bated him.

'It's not my car.'

'Then whose car is it?'

'Hans'.'

'Hans Zimmer gave you his Porsche?'

The Painter finally opened the door. Emily took the key from his hand. 'No way am I getting in a car with you. Look at the state of you. The police would probably pull us over in a second and I'm not convinced you're insured for this car. I'm not even sure that it's not stolen. I can't see Hans Zimmer giving anyone his car.' Emily shook her head. 'Shit.'

As a taxi made its way slowly down the street she shot her right hand out and grabbed The Painter with her left. The cab pulled over and Emily opened the back door, dragging The Painter in after her.

Inside the taxi she looked at his face. His eyes were closed and his breathing regular. He had fallen asleep.

The thud of the glass against his left temple startled The Painter, before he pitched forwards in his seat and landed on the floor of the taxi.

His first view was of Emily's feet and legs. He noticed immediately how neatly the laces on her boots were tied. Her legs were thin but still held a curved shape at the shins. The car was stationary and Emily was paying the driver.

The Painter crawled around to Emily's feet. He smelled the freshly polished, pointed toe of her boot. It was new and entirely without creases. He pushed his tongue between the first gap in the ladder of her laces. He then bumped it up the tight leather strings until he reached the looped end at the top of her ankles. He bit into the leather lace and pulled it along his tongue. It left a slightly stringent taste in his mouth. He raised his head and spat out hard at the toe of the boot then began to arrange himself onto his haunches.

Emily kicked into the underside of The Painter's left armpit, pulling the boot hard under the woollen grain. She dropped her foot back before raising it again and wiping it along the underside of his left sleeve.

'Fucking artists,' the taxi driver mouthed, as Emily regained her composure and alighted from the cab, followed by the stumbling painter.

Once on the pavement she turned to him with disconsolate eyes. She momentarily caught her countenance in a window before turning again to him. 'For God's sake just try and act sober, or give the impression that you have some control over your limbs,' she cautioned with exasperation.

The Painter's eyes searched up and down either side of the street. It was nestled perfectly between two larger roads at either side. The parked cars were all a sedate black and grey, except for two low-slung, sporty versions, one of which was a vibrant red and the other orange. The shop fronts were in perfect symmetry with their environment. They were black and white and cream and grey. Some had discrete awnings and small topiaried trees outside their doorways. They had names such as Bulgari, Cartier, Prada, Gucci, Dior, Hermes. At the corner was a restaurant called Tangerine, which had two small orange trees standing to attention at either side of its chic doorway.

Up above the large, minimal glass frontage of the building they stood in front of was the lone title 'Francesca Spilotti', scripted in a fashionable black font. The rest of the building was painted in an elegant off-white that looked like cream but probably had a much more complex and expensive name.

Emily took hold of The Painter, looping her left arm through his right. She pressed him firmly towards the entrance of the building and pushed the thick glass doors open in a stubbornly effortless manner.

Standing just inside the doorway was a tall, burly man; well-dressed, head to toe in black. He smiled warily at the couple as they entered the reception area. Emily stealthily opened her handbag and produced two white cards.

'The exhibition is through there,' he motioned towards the gallery space. Emily moved swiftly onwards without acknowledgement, stealing The Painter once more with her.

As they went towards the exhibition space, The Painter noticed that above the entrance, written in multi-coloured neon light were the words: 'It's all about me me me'. The word 'It's' was coloured red, 'all' pink, 'about' yellow, while the first 'me' was orange, the second violet, and the third turquoise. On the white wall next to the entrance was stated: *Samantha Kilgore: My First Ever Retrospective.*

The Painter peeled away from Emily and moved towards the wording on the wall. He spied on them at point-blank range. He checked the angles from the sides. The etching showed no signs of physical differentiation from the white painted plaster. He made to smell the wall, when Emily interceded. She yanked him briskly away by his right hand and The Painter reluctantly followed, like a badly-behaved Labrador puppy.

The pair moved into one of the main gallery spaces. The walls were of a pure brilliantine white and the ceiling held a raft of specialist lighting, featuring spots of various compositions. The room was large and spacious and already contained a buzzing crowd, some of whom mulled around the artworks on display while others swooned around each other. The most incongruous element of all in the room was the giant, taxidermied, giraffe's head.

A young woman dressed entirely in black, with long, straight, blonde hair, a pretty smile and impeccable manners, ambled past The Painter and Emily, proffering glasses of champagne from a silver tray. Emily pulled two from the tray and handed one to The Painter.

'For god's sake, try and eat something before drinking that,' she cautioned The Painter quietly. 'And don't touch any of the artworks.'

With that, Emily peeled away from The Painter

towards an attractive dark-haired woman, who was wearing a blue dress with a lushly soft red wrap which draped round her back and came to rest on her elbows.

The two women stood apart from one another until the older woman had finished her conversation with a distinguished-looking bald gentleman in brown trousers and a tweed jacket. When the man parted company from the woman, she signalled to Emily to approach. 'These academics are such a frightful bore, but he might write a piece in the *Journal of Contemporary Aesthetics* for her.'

Emily lifted her eyebrows. 'That should be fun to read.' She took a first sip of her champagne.

'Oh god, don't,' Francesca replied, before sighing. 'How the hell did I get myself into this game?' She looked across at The Painter standing on his own, staring at the giraffe's head and drinking his champagne. 'Well, how is he? He looks stoned.' She looked back at Emily. 'Is he stoned?'

'I don't know what he is. He hasn't taken anything since I've been with him. I can't vouch for earlier.'

'Did you tell him about the sale of his painting today?'

'Yes.'

'And?'

'Nothing. Nothing at all.'

Francesca turned to Emily and stared at her for a moment, then turned away towards the centre of the room again, eyes scanning the space for important guests. 'He didn't even ask how much it went for?'

'No.'

'Did you tell him?'

'No. Should I have?' Emily looked now at the woman.

'No, that's fine. I'm sure he'll get around to it eventually. Then he'll bitch about the price and our percentage.'

The two women faced each other.

'You have a future in this game,' the woman finally

gave Emily her full attention. 'You know your business well. That was a good sale. A tough sale. I've dealt with him before. He's not easily parted from his money. In spite of how much of it he's got.'

'That's always the way,' Emily replied.

They both returned to watching the room.

'They're trouble, you know,' the woman stated.

'Who?'

'Artists.'

'I can live with it.'

'They're a pain in the arse. Always wanting something. Like spoilt children.'

'I can handle them.'

'I don't doubt it. I've seen you work. A word of caution, though, stick to the business side of it.'

'What do you mean?'

'What do I mean?' She sounded surprised. 'A red-headed temptress, intelligent and sexy? They'll all want to fuck you. The suppliers and the buyers alike: boys and girls. I've been there too, you know. I've made my mistakes.' Francesca watched The Painter move through the gallery. 'Is he drunk?'

'I don't know.'

'Don't let him drink too much.'

'He won't listen to me.'

'I'm sure you can be perfectly persuasive when you want to be.'

They stood quietly together for a few minutes, simply watching The Painter.

Emily broke the silence, 'I had to shave him earlier.'

The older woman shook her head. 'Fucking infants.'

'He wants his key back.'

The woman turned to Emily. 'To the studio?'

'Yes.'

'You didn't give it to him.'

'Of course not.'

The woman eyed Emily suspiciously. 'Okay. Good.'

A well-dressed, middle-aged man called out, 'Francesca!' The older woman glided off with an extravagant greeting.

The Painter stared disconsolately at the giraffe's head. He had been gradually edging his way towards it since Emily had disappeared to speak to the matronly guardian of the room.

Its eyes were large and black and viciously dead. The fur which covered the head bristled in the light. The two large ossicones protruding from its skull reached towards the high ceiling. Its orange and brown patches were neatly shaped and separated by a faun-coloured, structurally patterned, outline. The head and neck were pinned resolutely to a giant plinth. There was no gore, or blade markings, to show off the decapitation.

The Painter wondered what was inside. He wanted to push his own head up into the giraffe. The flesh and bone scooped out and replaced with a polyurethane form. A grossly weird overcoat of skin and fur: the eyeballs and vertebrae missing. A vacuum of decay, pampered and stuffed. The Painter viewed an oversized, rough-hewn rug, lying vacant on the polished concrete of the gallery floor. What did it mean?

CHAPTER 10

A heavy, loose arm placed itself on The Painter's shoulder. There was a musky smell of aftershave and the polish of minty breath.

'Hello again, my friend. So nice to see you so soon after we last met.'

The Painter turned to face the stubbly, white-toothed grin of Urs, who dropped his arm and swigged his champagne.

'Some rough pigswill from the local supermarket, no doubt,' Urs offered by explanation of his now empty glass. 'These people are always cheap.'

'Who?' The Painter asked.

'Them.' Urs nodded towards the woman in the blue dress who Emily had spoken to. She was now standing next to a tall, slim, silver-haired, suntanned man. 'Your gallerist, Francesca Spilotti, and her husband Stephen Cornell-Jones, of the venerable jewellers.'

'Jewellers?'

Urs looked at The Painter, puzzled. 'You didn't know he was related to the famous jewellers? Grandson of the founder. There you go, my friend, success personified. And yet they don't know a pinot noir from a monkey's piss. They're probably both on the edge of bankruptcy.'

The Painter looked around the gallery. Urs watched keenly.

'Don't be fooled by this glittering bauble. A simple chimera, that's all. A fucking mirage. Not even that clever. A ruse to defraud.' Urs laughed a little. 'And probably you, my friend.'

'Me?'

'I heard you sold a painting today. To a very important client. Had your cheque yet?'

'Cheque?'

'No, I thought not. I'm telling you, my friend, it's a dirty business. That's why I keep my hands clean.'

'Why are you here?'

'You don't know?'

'No.'

'To see you, my friend.' Urs grabbed himself another champagne and one for The Painter. The young man dressed all in black, who served them, smiled at Urs. 'I've had him,' Urs remarked. 'Not bad. A good solid seven. Anyway, where was I? Ah yes, Hans. Have you seen Hans yet, since we last spoke?'

'Hans? No.'

'I really need to speak to him. You see. Well, I wasn't exactly honest with you the last time we spoke. You know about China. The truth is, I have my own Asian contacts and Hans' aren't worth shit to me. He has, however, acquired a certain item I wish to get my hands on.'

'A painting?'

Urs looked at The Painter with a mixture of disbelief and contempt. 'Do I exist in a different fucking realm of the universe to you, my friend? Didn't we have a conversation about this already? I don't collect paintings. I don't collect art. I collect objects of beauty. Hans has purchased an object of design which I covet greatly. It's a piece by an old French woman that came onto the market recently. It was previously owned by one of these fashion house guys and Hans' wife happens to be a good client of this couture guru and so she set up the sale for him and in the process gazumped me. I strongly suspect the only reason Hans wanted the piece was to rub my face in it.'

'Rub your face in it?'

'Okay, I admit, I occasionally dabble in the art market, but only for financial reasons, not for aesthetic interests. I've fenced, so to speak, a few bits and pieces here and there for other people. People who wish to remain anonymous. As such, I occasionally step on the toes of some collectors. This may be one such case. However, Hans and I are both rational businessmen and I'm sure we can come to a sensible arrangement; one that's mutually beneficial to both of us. Now, it happens a certain photograph is about to enter the market. A piece Hans may well be interested in acquiring and I am in the fortuitous position to effect a purchase for him,' Urs paused, shrugged delicately, 'in exchange for this piece of furniture I'm referring to. You see, my friend, the owner of the photograph is a manic bibliophile and I happen to have stumbled upon a very rare manuscript by a Russian poet, banned under both the Csar and the Bolsheviks, that he's willing to part-exchange for the photograph. I just need to throw him a little financial sweetener on the side to make the whole deal worth it. I'm willing to do this, but I need Hans' authority to proceed. Otherwise I'm going to be left out of pocket, holding the baby, so to speak. I'm not the baby-holding type, you see. So, there is the complete tale. I've told you everything. Naturally there's a little finder's fee in it for you, my friend. After all, we're not fucking Bolsheviks, are we?' He looked The Painter up and down, assessing him. 'Of course, you may be. Some of you artists are. That's okay, it's your prerogative and all that. If it makes you feel better, give the money to one of your causes. Ban the bomb and save the poor, or some such shit.'

'The bomb?'

'Whatever the latest cause du jour with you lot is.' Urs spied someone across the room. 'I must be running along. I'm taking Rudi dancing later. But, right now I've got a spot of business to transact. Keep in touch, my friend. And don't drink too much of this fucking gut-rot.' He placed his empty glass on a passing tray and disappeared into the massing crowd.

The Painter turned his attention towards a large photograph on the wall to his left. He walked over to view it more closely. In it a woman was bound tightly from head to toe in cling-film. Her breasts and nose appeared painfully squashed out of shape. The only part of her anatomy not covered was her mouth, which was left open wide. Her lips were coloured in a violently red lipstick. The title next to the artwork was simply: *Girlfriend*.

The hole in her mouth formed a strange void. Her teeth and tongue and throat were not visible. There was simply a red circle filled with black. The Painter felt erotically stirred by the image and deeply horrified. He moved his left index finger out instinctively towards the picture and that dark, cavernous space. His hand recoiled from the attempt at union. The mouth was hostile: it could bite his finger, break it, snap it off. There could be anything in the hole. It was a deep, black, infinite shadow. It could devour a whole hand. It could grip him and never relinquish its hold.

Instead, The Painter touched the cool, clean blankness of the wall. He pushed his hand along it for a couple of metres. His eyes closed and he felt the stark whiteness projected from his vision of the wall blend with the natural blackness of his blind sight. He could feel no texture nor grain on the wall. He was no longer tethered to the physical world. The wall held him stable but he could no longer discern its presence. When he finally opened his eyes again he stumbled against a man's arm, causing him to spill some champagne. The man stared at him, awaiting an apology. The Painter glanced down at the spilled wine. He was attempting to bend down on his knees to examine it when he was pulled upwards by an invisible hand.

'Darling, how are you? You made it.' Francesca Spilotti took hold of The Painter and kissed him on both cheeks. 'What do you think? Isn't it wonderful? She's going to be a star.' Francesca had wrapped her right arm tightly around The Painter's left and was ushering him across the room towards the opposite wall.

For the first time, The Painter could see Francesca closely. Her eyes were a warm brown, brows plucked into perfect arches and lashes cautiously darkened. She had a long, thin nose, sharp cheekbones, and a neatly defined jawline and chin. Her skin tones were subtle: a hint of light brown and pink. The flesh was blemish-free and projected a healthy radiance. She smiled without effort and her mild pink lipstick set her perfect teeth off with a mannered grace. She wore a silver sculptural necklace that held together without either end touching. The Painter might have placed her in her mid-thirties until he looked at her neckline. There were small but significant creases growing along it. He wanted to kiss and nip them with his teeth, to find out if they were real. If she squealed he would let her go.

Francesca looked closely at The Painter's face. 'Darling, you look dreadful. You're working too much. That's why I sent Emily around to collect you and bring you out for some fun. You have some cause for celebration, too. Did Emily tell you we sold one of your paintings today? It was a good sale. I'll have your payment sent through in the next few days. The financial arrangements are a bit complicated, as you can imagine. I'll have it sorted out soon. Market fluctuations and currency exchange and all that. No need for me to bore you with the details. You must eat something, though. Keep up your strength for the painting. Have you seen the whole show? Take a good look. We'll catch up later, perhaps have a little supper.'

Without pausing for his concurrence, Francesca disappeared as quickly as she arrived.

The Painter turned to the artworks hanging on the wall. Scattered across the white space were photographs of the woman he had seen wrapped in cling-film, but this time in various poses with the giraffe's head. In one she wore cute pyjamas, snuggled up in bed with the head, which was evidently called Jeff. In another photo, her arms were flung around Jeff's neck in a display of great affection.

The young woman with blonde hair popped up next to The Painter, offering a tray of canapés.

'What is it?'

'Scottish smoked salmon, crème fraiche, with a Spanish olive on a crostini.' The girl smiled.

The Painter looked at the pinkish slither of fish which had been skinned and gutted, beheaded and smothered. It had been drowned and decapitated, its innards drawn out, then a fire lit under it. He touched the fish. It was cool and moist to the touch: the fresh mountain water had been wrung from its core. The Painter shook his head. His behaviour seemed objectionable to the girl with the blonde hair. She removed the food he had touched, wrapped it in a napkin, and passed on without comment.

'Fucking awful, isn't it?'

The Painter turned towards the voice. Dan Smithson was standing next to him, attired in black skinny jeans, black-and-white chequered trainers, black-and-white striped top, grey jacket, and grey pork pie hat.

'The art?' The Painter asked.

'The food,' Smithson offered as he threw back two canapés.

'The food?'

'Yeah, it's always the same at these things. Fucking tapenades and roulades, hors d'oeuvres, canapés, amuse-bouches and sushi. Some rotten shit smeared over a piece of overpriced toast, conjured up by some kid straight out of catering school who thinks he's got two Michelin stars under his belt already. I don't honestly think people like eating this crap. I've never understood why they don't lay on proper grub like samosas, pakora and onion bhajis. People want fun food; slightly exotic but substantial, like spring rolls and mini pizzas. I suppose it's about the art at the end of the day. These are just a slight distraction. And

God knows it needs it,' he helped himself to some more food. 'Awful, just awful.'

'The food?' The Painter asked again.

'The art,' Smithson clarified. 'Another rising star of the art world. She's fucking blown it already. I saw her MA show. I was an external examiner for it. That work had bite and wit. And this,' he made a vague sweeping gesture with his hand. 'Some fucking nonsense about losing her favourite soft toy while on a trip to Kenya with her parents as a child. And that's it. That is fucking it.'

'What?'

'The entirety of western civilisation, through all of those upheavals: wars and pestilence and famine and plague and despots and kings and queens and emperors and popes and dictators and madmen and revolutions and reforms and enterprises and expeditions and empires and science and technology and weaponry and art and barbarism and enlightenment and communes and castles. All of it reduced down to a fucking child's cuddly toy named Jeff. I've completely wasted that PhD. I've completely wasted my fucking life,' Dan Smithson shook his head. 'And there's even more of this shit next door. Along with the artist. She asked me if I'd be writing a piece about her. I'll do her a favour and not bother. Speaking of which, did you read that piece I wrote for you yet?'

'The piece?'

'Yeah, man, the piece I wrote for you in *Art and Culture*. You haven't seen it yet?'

'I saw it.'

'Well, what do you think?'

'Think? I don't know.'

'Christ, you artists don't want much, do you? That was a really good piece. I heard you sold a painting today. I'd like to think that article contributed in its own small but significant way to that sale.'

The young man went past, serving glasses of

champagne. Dan Smithson snatched two and handed one to The Painter.

'Here, get that down your throat,' he took a hard look at The Painter. 'Man, you look like shit. I mean, you look even worse than you did last night. Did you manage to get in a fight on the way home or something?'

'No. I had an accident.'

'I'll say. Slipped and fell on your razor blade, did you? You're a clumsy bastard. So what do you think?'

'About what?'

'About what. The Siberian. Have you been to see him yet?'

'No.'

'Jesus fucking Christ, man. This guy is going to fuck me up. I thought you said you would speak to him.'

'Okay.'

'When?'

'Tomorrow.'

'If you don't, you realise I'm a dead man. And not in a nice way, either.'

'Okay.'

'I mean, of course, I'll see you right over time.'

'See me right?'

'Sure, about the money. But you know I've got a whole lot of articles left in me like that last one,' Dan Smithson spoke proudly. 'We could sell loads more pictures. You paint them and I'll write them up. I've got a new blog going. Have you seen it?'

'No.'

'I'll send you a link, along with The Siberian's address again, in case you've lost it or deleted it or something. Hey, did I see you talking to Urs von Madsen earlier on?'

'Urs? Yes, Urs.'

'What was that stubbly whale after? Trying to reamer your arse, no doubt. You know that guy's fucked every waiter and barman in this town. I think he's got a thing for uniforms. Don't suppose he's got a hard-on for artists, though.'

'He doesn't like art.'

'Doesn't like art. Let me tell you something about Urs von Madsen, mate. He likes anything that you can hang a price tag around, especially if it's a price tag that leans towards his percentage. Von, my arse. Stay away from him, he's trouble. They're all trouble. That dealer of yours and her sleazy fuck husband.' Dan watched Francesca work the room, smiling, waving, eyeing up the waiters as they circled with bottles. 'These people don't give a shit about you. They'll push your price up until you can't sell any more then they'll flood the market with your work. They'll be quids-in and you'll be ruined. These fuckers do deals with everyone. All kinds of unsavoury cats. You'll be watching the news one day and you'll see one of your paintings hanging up in some far-flung dictator's palace when the masses turn up to ransack the joint. Most of your paintings are probably propping up some warehouse at an airport in Switzerland. Think about Swiss moral rectitude when it comes to artworks. One word: Nazis. Say no more. Who knows who really goes shopping in these galleries? Know who bought your painting today?'

'No.'

'I've heard some rumours. I had lunch with a well-connected curator today, who threw out a couple of names. Won't help you sleep at night, though.'

The Painter held his hands over his eyes and closed them. He could feel his soft breathing through his nostrils. The terminal chatter throughout the space dissipated. The mouths and words were merging and diluting. The air surrounding him was becoming volumeless.

'I need your help,' Dan Smithson continued talking, seemingly unaware of The Painter's internal struggle, too concerned with his own problems. 'I need fifty grand to get this Siberian bastard off my back and you can do it.

I'm counting on you. You're all I've got. I can make a career. Christ, I made yours, didn't I? And I can do it again. You can have critical success as well as commercial success. Go and see him, please. I'll make it worth it. I make a good ally,' he leaned in close and whispered, 'and a real shit for an enemy.'

The Painter dropped his hand and looked at Smithson.

'What is that, a migraine or something?' Smithson noticed The Painter's pallor. 'You should get yourself to a doctor, mate.' The critic shook his head. 'Anyway, I'm going to leave now. I've got a hot date later with my lady friend. Take it easy and go and see The Siberian. Please.'

Dan Smithson placed his empty champagne flute on a passing tray and left. On his way out he passed Emily. He tipped his ridiculous pork pie hat to her in a gentlemanly manner before exiting the gallery, laughing gaily.

Emily had posted her best plastic smile for him and raised her glass a touch in salute. She stood scanning the room: drinking in the ambience. Watching the swirling, animated crowd chattering about art, politics, business, fashion, restaurants, parties, properties, and the distant metropolis. People clung to one another; some superior, some confident, some arrogant, some elegant, some edgy, some sincere. She stood apart, alone, conscious of the game and the important part she had to play in it. Her world, the world of art, of the gallery, of the media. The world of business and relationships and deals and power and money.

She hadn't noticed the figure standing next to her. Francesca and Emily stood side by side, staring out over the evening, one pensive and the other smiling softly.

'What do you think?' Francesca asked.

'It's a good crowd,' Emily answered carefully.

'It's Monday night. There's nothing else going on. The crowd doesn't matter. The reviews are important, but most important of all are the players. There are a few here tonight. We might make something of it.' Sometimes Francesca enjoyed playing the role of the pedagogue. But not for long.

'There's a nice buzz about the place. The food's good.'

'A new caterer. Young lad. He'll go far. Like you.'

'Me,' Emily turned to Francesca in surprise.

'Don't be so shocked. It's in your blood. I was watching you standing here, aloof, surveying the domain. You reminded me of me.'

'I like to watch people, observe them.'

'Talking of which, I witnessed our friend talking to that creep Dan Smithson.'

'He wrote a good piece for him in *Art and Culture*.'

'I know, that's what worries me. I didn't care for that article at all.'

'Why?'

'Because I don't trust him. He's after something. I don't know what. That man does nothing for nothing.'

'Do you want me to try and find out what he's after?'

'No, don't worry I'll take care of that.' Francesca watched the room for a moment, zeroing in on The Painter as he held his face close to a bare stretch of wall. 'What I would like you to do is make sure our little genius gets home okay. He looks like he's been hit by a bus. I need him fighting fit and in good shape.'

Emily looked over to her right. 'Who's that man over there with the stubbly face? You were talking to him earlier. I feel I recognise him.'

Francesca looked over. 'Oh him, that's Urs von Madsen. He's a real wheeler and dealer. He's got his finger in every pie going. He's as slippery as they come, but he knows an awful lot of people.'

'He seems to know every waiter and barman in town, from what I've heard.'

'He likes them young and buff. He's shacked up with some pretty boy at the moment. Claims he's going to make him a pop star.'

'Good luck with that.'

'Don't bet against him. He usually gets what he wants. One way or another.'

'Don't they all.'

Both women watched The Painter move through into the other part of the gallery.

'Go and look after him, will you? Make sure he doesn't break anything. And for God's sake don't let him talk to the press. Grab a taxi and get him home as soon as you can.'

'He tried to bring me here in a Porsche.'

Francesca turned to her. 'A Porsche? He's bought a Porsche? I didn't even know he could drive.'

'It's not his. Hans Zimmer gave it to him.'

'Hans Zimmer gave him a Porsche?'

'So he says.'

'That's a dubious story. I can't see Hans Zimmer doing that.'

'Well, he's got a Porsche from somewhere. I've seen it.'

'I hope it's not stolen. That boy doesn't half get himself in some scrapes. Still, I suppose it's good for his image. And what's good for him is good for us,' Francesca's body language changed. 'I'd better get back to my husband before he starts complaining I abandoned him all night to boring, dull people.'

Francesca abandoned Emily, leaving her to go and search out The Painter and fulfil her duties.

CHAPTER 11

The gallery was split into two large exhibition spaces. The second room was slightly larger than the first. It was rectangular in shape, with the ubiquitous white-washed walls and highly buffed concrete floors. The lighting changed from the first to the second gallery space, where it was given off by a single central bank of large diffuse white ceiling lights.

The Painter glanced around the room aimlessly, trying to effect some kind of bearing. He looked back at the connecting entrance between the two spaces and tried to discern the difference. The two rooms appeared the same. The people crowding the second room looked like the same people that had inhabited the first. The mumbling chatter, the handshakes, the kisses, the laughter, the hushed reverence, were all familiar from the other exhibition space. The lynchpin of orientation in this room, though, was the black grand piano placed in the centre.

The Painter read the placard on the wall which stated the piece was entitled *Penetration*. He moved slowly towards the piece, parting guests and patrons along the way. Some people inevitably recognised him and responded by saying hello, nodding, or gesturing in some way. The Painter ignored them all.

Eventually, when in full view of the piece, he dropped onto all fours and began to crawl towards it. He had noticed something about the work from a distance. Its core artistic element was on the underside.

The guts of the piano had been eviscerated and were strewn all around the floor underneath it. The wires had been cut and striated everywhere. The keys had been pulled through the piano's belly and were scattered around the floor. The encompassing scene was a scatological jumble of piano keys, both black and white, piano wires, and fragments of broken wood.

The Painter crawled in amongst the debris and lay on his back to stare up into the undercarriage of the musical instrument. Right in the centre of its underbelly a large, perfectly round hole had been cut where the debris protruded. He stared up into the darkness inside. The piano was no longer playable. He raised his arms up in an attempt to enter. Unaware of the encroaching crowd.

'I don't think you should be doing that,' a female voice from overhead echoed through the hole he was trying to enter. The Painter managed to wheel himself free of the piano's shadow and lift himself up.

A middle-aged woman in a black dress, wearing black shoes and holding a red handbag, was standing at the centre of the crowd which had gathered to watch, unsure if it was a performance, a part of the art.

'I think you should respect an artist's work,' the woman stated boldly.

'He is an artist,' came an anonymous male voice from the back of the crowd.

'All the more reason to respect a fellow artist's work,' she replied, unwilling to be diverted by the intrusion.

The Painter glanced at all the concerned faces before staring directly at the woman, who seemed to be expecting trouble from him. 'Sorry,' he quietly said and promptly moved away from the scene.

Towards the back of the room stood a man in his mid-thirties, dressed in a grey suit, black shoes and blue open-collared shirt. He held a small digital recorder with a stubby microphone protruding from one end. The man was holding it out towards a young woman in her late twenties. She had short black hair, tight black leggings, high wedge-heeled shoes, a black lace top and black leather jacket. The woman wore little make-up, which accentuated her natural allure. The Painter recognised her from the photographs; she was the artist Samantha Kilgore, and this was her show.

On the back wall of the gallery, a grid of photographs hung in white box frames. The grid pattern was made up of ten photos by ten photos: 100 photographs in total. The Painter was drawn towards them, magnetised by the display. Each photograph contained a sonogram image of a gestating foetus. Each a picture of a different chid. The Painter drew close to one and marvelled at the illuminated black-and-white image, until seeing was no longer enough. He moved his fingers around, tracing the outline of the womb. He closed his eyes and saw swirling monochrome patterns; a cartoon world of giant panoramic friezes of miscellaneous abstract doodles. They rushed passed his mind's eye and merged and danced around the inside of his closed eyelids.

The Painter stood further back from the work. The white of the frames and the wall, the chiaroscuro images held within the frames, glimmered. He looked at the title: *All the babies I could have gotten by you if it wasn't for the wonder of contraception.* He viewed again the vaguely formed anthropomorphic shape, the sweeping lines; no heartbeat, no pulse, just shapes and forms and shadows and light.

Samantha Kilgore was speaking to the journalist. 'I think the term "feminist" is always bandied about by the media when the work is presented by a female artist; it just seems to be de rigueur. Not that I mind the term, nor want to disassociate myself from it, but it always feels to me a rather narrow rendering of the focus of the work.'

'What would you say the focus of the work was, then?' the journalist asked.

'I honestly think of the pieces on display as being essentially biographical and diaristic. Being a woman naturally means some broader feministic concerns are brought to the fore. But that is not necessarily the essence of the meaning behind the pieces themselves.'

'But, like you say, there is going to be some feminist

residue produced by the work.'

'Absolutely, I totally accept that, but it still isn't the main thrust of the work. Each and every piece is separate. For instance, there is nothing remotely feminist surrounding the piece about the giraffe. Whereas understandably there are feminist overtures in other pieces such as *Girlfriend* and perhaps a merging of the personal and the feminist in a work such as *Penetration*.'

'Can we actually talk about that piece a little, because it's quite a strange and obscure work, especially the title. Can you explain it for me?'

'When I was young, a teenager, I decided I wanted to learn to play the piano. So, I arranged to take private lessons, which I paid for myself by taking on a few different jobs, including a paper round. I took an hour's lesson every week for about nine months, before I got bored, really, and I also realised I wasn't very musically gifted. Now it happens that the man who gave me the lessons was some years later investigated by the police for being inappropriate with some students. I don't think he was ever actually charged with anything, but there were a number of allegations made against him. When I heard this, from my mother, I racked my brain to think of any instances when he may have been inappropriate with me and I couldn't think of any. Then I began to question my own memory and whether or not I had repressed any traumas associated with my piano lessons. It all became so suggestive for me. I really doubted myself. Then I began to realise that it was around the same age, about thirteen or fourteen, that I had my first kiss and first slightly awkward relationship with a boy. I think it only lasted about two school discos, but it was still significant. And so I came to associate the piano, this inanimate musical instrument, with my sexual development and all the complexities and quandaries that involves.'

'It feels like a very violent piece. What you've just

described is a somewhat vague and slightly irrational response to the stuff of life. The awkwardness of youth, the apprehension of criminal behaviour.'

'But it is the stuff of life,' the artist was enthusiastic, clearly pleased with this opening. 'I'm not sure what really went on with this piano teacher. I'm certain he was innocent of any misdoings with regard to me. This teenage boy was innocent, too; if anything, I had to coax him into the kiss. Yet the wider concerns remain. The world of adolescence for a girl and a boy is a complex and sometimes dangerous place to manoeuvre through. It certainly remains that way for women, from workplace harassment, to domestic abuse, to rape and murder. The world is fraught with danger, much of which is generated from sex. Nothing happened to me, but it could so easily have done. I doubt very much that many women pass through life without at least one uncomfortable experience of a sexual nature, even it's just being wolf-whistled by a bunch of builders when you're walking down the street.'

'So you can't really separate your work entirely from a feminist perspective?'

'Well, no, I suppose not, if you want to make the point.' Her enthusiasm wavered. He had returned to feminism.

'You're uncomfortable with it, though. A little, at least,' he surmised.

'I don't think any artist wants to regard their work as having a narrow focus. I mean, it's a case of the old adage that through the particular we can discover something of the universal; the personal is always political. I want my work to have a broad appeal, that's all. I think a work can be either feminine or macho or anything else, but can still have validity outside of those concerns. Take Willem de Kooning. I find his portraits of women thoroughly misogynistic, almost homicidal, but I still love viewing them, because I'm interested in the technique, his painterly style, rather than the subject matter.'

'So, in the end, it's a show as much for men as it is for women.'

'Absolutely.'

'Do you feel it's significant that you're represented by a gallery owned by a woman?'

'I don't think that's anything to do with it really,' the artist began to flag, but she maintained a professional stance. 'Francesca represents a wide variety of top international artists. It's a great stable with great pedigree. She represents female and male artists. I think the one thing we all have in common is the quality of the work. Women have always played an active role in the arts. There are plenty of galleries today owned by women, run by women and curated by women, but on behalf of everyone, male and female. Perhaps it's a more feminist extension of the patronage that was always there from Catherine de Medici to the old salon system. Of course, most of the artists who benefitted were, in fact, men.'

The Painter wandered along the walls of the room, examining other framed, photographic prints. One featured an operating theatre, where a surgeon was cutting open a female breast. Its title: *Bad Genes (mastectomy)*. The medical staff wore pale green scrubs. The scalpel glittered and glistened with blood. The flesh of the soft white breast had been neatly sliced open. The Painter moved his hand towards the deep red wound. His stomach felt queasy and pins and needles ran up and down his legs. He noticed people walked past the image; he was the only guest viewing the print. He moved on to the next photograph; a black-and-white self-portrait of Samantha Kilgore with the title *Bad Genes (chemotherapy)*. An unemotional woman stared unflinchingly at the camera. Her head was bald and her eyebrows ostentatiously pencilled in. Further along the same wall was a third and final photograph called *Bad Genes (infinity)*. This piece was in colour and set in a church graveyard. Central to the image was a gravestone, carved onto which were the words: 'Samantha Jane Kilgore. Artist. Died 33 Years Of Age'.

The Painter looked into the photograph then looked across the room at the artist still talking to the journalist. Under her top, beneath the bra, was half a breast and raw, sewn-up scar tissue. The other half had been discarded: examined and incinerated. Flesh reduced to ash and spread into the air in a plume of smoke. Were her hair and eyebrows wigs? Stuck on to mimic that which had been lost? Was it even true? Perhaps Samantha Kilgore was dead, a ghost stalking the gallery floor, giving out quotes to an on-hand media. He wanted to meet her, touch her skin, feel the naked flesh under her wig, trace the draughtsman's pencil-line along her brows. Her hair looked real; the breasts looked whole. The photograph in the operating theatre was an illusion. The artist was not in the shot. It need not have been a real operation, in a real hospital; it could have been fake, just make-up and actors, in a studio. He stared hard at the photographs. What was real and what was fake? He didn't know. Perhaps that was the artist's purpose.

The Painter felt a sharp pain in his stomach. He crouched over slightly and placed his half-empty champagne flute on the floor. He began to backtrack through the gallery to a staircase grandly placed in between the entrance to both spaces. The Painter pulled himself up the stairs. Each leaden foot following on from the last. The eyes starting to drown in their own vapour: the focus becoming incomplete.

The Painter stopped on the landing and leaned his head on the broad banister. It was topped with dark, polished wood, intricately grained. He stared into the tight weave of the grain, with its deep rhythms and knots. The wood smelled of fresh, waxy polish; a smell The Painter found both distressing and comforting. He smeared his tongue along it until it was dry and raw. The trail of saliva, which he had laid, was evaporating almost instantaneously on the non-porous surface. The moisture filtered into the atmosphere.

The Painter continued onwards to the top of the stairs. To his left was a large, darkened exhibition space. The remnants of a previous show were still on offer but no longer palatable. There were wooden crates scattered around in the pale gloom of the dying light. He stood and stared into the room. He felt an air of desolation as he searched his fading memory for a link to the gallery space; it all seemed depressingly familiar but incohesive. There was an air of inevitability about those walls. He moved towards them, compelled to touch their surface, feel that open neutrality held within. His hands could feel their blankness: their cool, smooth skin. Untainted by any art, or design, or any other wall-hangings. He couldn't bear it. The Painter spat out across them, he punched the wall as hard as he could with his left fist. The streak of blood scarred the pristine whiteness. He wiped the back of his hand to and fro along the wall's surface. He searched the room for anything immediate and sharp. He could find nothing. There were windows at the end of the room but he had no energy to run at them. He could not have forced himself through them.

The Painter turned to the corridor adjacent to the exhibition space. He could feel his bladder beginning to empty, as a trickle of urine seeped into his shorts. He rushed towards a door marked with a basic line drawing of a woman. He crashed into the toilet, before detaching his trousers and urinating in a sink. He moaned a little to himself as a full stream of yellow liquid poured into the white enamel bowl. The syrupy piss swilled around the edges of the sink before going down the plughole. The end of The Painter's penis stung slightly as he finished and shook it mildly. He lifted his fingers to his nose and smelled the strong, acidic scent.

There was a man trapped in the mirror, staring out dementedly at The Painter. An image with an unhinged glimmer of absolute decay; of a body and mind falling away.

He pulled his trousers back up and squelched mildly in his damp shorts.

The Painter stared down into the black recesses of the plughole. It seemed to open itself up, the guards peeling their way back to leave a gaping hole. The voice he heard was blankly neutral. 'There is only you, and you alone. You are contained within yourself.'

He wanted to follow the trailing noise down through the dark, cavernous hole. To squeeze through into an ever-expanding abyss.

The Painter touched his fingers down into the sink. He tried to flick the final vestiges of his kidneys into the emergent blackness. He wondered, if he pierced the sink with his hand, how far down it would lead him. Would the sink retaliate and retract itself inwards, ripping his arm off? The blood would pour and swish around the floor tiles. Gushing along the seams of grout. Streaming down the white, transient walls of the gallery space below. Absorbed into the lightest pores of that most impenetrable of skins.

The toilet door swung open and The Painter raised his eyes high enough to catch the reflection of Emily in the mirror. She stood for a moment looking back at him, returning his gaze. 'There you are. I've been trying to find you. How are you holding up?'

The Painter didn't have the energy to reply.

Emily smiled and then laughed a little. 'You look worse every time I see you.'

As if to prove her point, The Painter began to retch. A small amount of brownish bile spattered over the bottom of the sink.

'How much have you had to drink?' Emily asked.

The Painter heaved again in answer.

'Have you eaten today?' Emily sounded more concerned.

She moved over to The Painter and stared into the sink. There were patterns of sluggish brown saliva covering its bleached white finish. She peeled off her right glove and swirled her index finger around the sink bottom, into the dregs of The Painter's stomach. She then held her finger up to her nose and smelled the brownish-yellow coating. She examined the muddy sheen covering her manicured finger. It clung to her clean, pink skin with a forensic disregard for her deeply moisturised pores. Emily turned on the tap with her left hand, squeezed the soap dispenser, and washed her soiled finger without comment. After replacing her glove, she walked over to the paper-towel dispenser and took one out.

The Painter looked at her sullenly as she wiped the vomit stains from around his mouth. She stared straight back into his eyes and then sniffed the air. 'There's always a smell of piss around you,' she stated, before bending her knees and sniffing The Painter's crotch.

He looked down at her glossy, thick red hair, sitting perfect on her head. Her boots laced tight against her slender ankles. He placed his hand timidly on her neck, at the point where it met the shoulder. He touched the skin, gently forming his fingertip along its smooth, creaseless surface. Her flesh was entirely unblemished. There was no tension or pain, no pimples or scald marks, no dirt or grime, no illness or disease. The Painter lifted his finger and looked at it, before holding it up to his nose. It had a fresh and vibrant citrus smell. A distillation of the pure essence of cool, precise beauty.

Emily was standing in front of him, her expression cold and unyielding. She walked over to a bin and disposed of the soiled paper towel. The Painter remained motionless.

'Come with me and I'll get you something to eat.' She held the door open for him to follow.

He walked past Emily and out into the corridor. He made to walk towards the stairway but was stopped by her voice. 'This way,' she stated, as she held open a door at the end of the corridor.

The Painter walked along the hallway, through a light grey door and into a large, bright, open plan office. There were two desks containing silver computer monitors, each with a separate keyboard and mouse. The only other item in common was a slim black telephone. The desk at the back was covered in papers and magazines. The one at the front was completely untouched. In the middle of the room, a large, square desk held a maquette of the exhibition spaces of the galleries downstairs. Detailed within it was the positioning of all of the pieces of art exhibited by Samantha Kilgore. There was a miniature grand piano, a scaled-down giraffe's head, and little figures representing the viewers. Along the right-side wall there was a large shelving unit containing rows of black-and-white box files. Along the left-side wall was shelving, containing row upon row of magazines and journals. Behind the desk at the back there were stacks of books of varying size and thickness. Pinned up on the front wall were sheets of white paper with details of Samantha Kilgore's exhibition marked out in thick, black pen. To the back of the room on the left was a closed door.

Emily stood behind the desk to the back right of the room. 'Come over here.'

She opened up a drawer in the desk and produced a packaged sandwich and a clear plastic bottle. The Painter stumbled faintly towards her, his vision relaxing to the point at which Emily seemed to be reproducing carbon copies of herself. He mustered enough strength to flop into her leather-and-chrome office chair. He wheeled back slightly as his mass effected the castors on the chair to push him towards the wall. Emily stopped the chair's movement with a swift flick of her heel on its base. She peeled back the plastic film which covered the sandwiches. Inside, two triangular halves of brown bread slices were filled with grilled chicken, salad and mayonnaise. She proffered one half to The Painter, who meekly accepted.

The quietness of the room struck him. The commotion of the exhibition downstairs was a distant murmur. The clean, purified air; the stark, bright lighting; the all-pervading whites and greys of the office reigned supreme. The classical harmony of Emily's presence elevated the room further. His dishevelled mess was at a dramatic variant to the natural balance inhabiting the space.

Emily gestured to the sandwich. 'It's not poisoned or out of date. I only bought it at lunchtime today.'

The Painter bit mournfully into the bread. He masticated the rubbery chicken and limp lettuce around in his mouth. The cloying paste of the mayonnaise struggled to liquefy the spongy bread. Emily watched his struggle with mild amusement before opening the bottle of sparkling mineral water and handing it to him. He grasped the bottle and glugged the contents greedily.

'Not too fast.' Emily's warning was drowned out as he choked, gargled, and spat the clump of half-ingested sandwich onto the floor.

Emily stared grimly at the ground. 'I think I preferred you when you were running around snorting cocaine from the bare arses of supermodels.'

'Supermodels?' The Painter asked, eyes filled with water.

'Not a hope in your state.' Emily began to wander around the room.

The Painter started a second attempt on the sandwich, alternating small mouthfuls with a sampling of water. He watched Emily closely as she ran her hands along the surfaces in a vague, distracted manner. She touched her desk, the central table, the other desk and the spines of magazines and books. She stared down into the spaces of the gallery model, moving the little figures around.

'I organised this exhibition, you know,' she said finally, moving towards the maquette.

'The one downstairs?' he continued to gently chew.

'I conceived it all. I even recommended her.'

'Who?'

'Samantha Kilgore. Francesca thinks it was her who first discovered Sam, at a minor exhibition she put on as part of an art residency she had at a hospital, but I had actually gone to Ms Kilgore's MA show. I knew she would be a star even then. Some people have a glow about them. You know, like they won't be touched by it all.'

'Touched?'

'By indecision, inertia, crises of confidence and self-esteem failure. Those types of things.'

'But aren't those types of things meant to be a part of art?'

'Oh, they sell well enough. They're good for a career, but they're largely inauthentic. All the artists we meet through these doors are arrogant pricks or automatons. It's all learned response, to teachers and tutors, critics and media, buyers and dealers, and eventually the public. Have an idea, one idea, and package it and repackage it and then flog it time and time again.'

The Painter kept eating while Emily stared into the gallery model on the table. She lifted her right fist up and made to smash it but stopped her hand just short of touching the top of the walls.

She turned wearily back to The Painter. 'I'm sorry, I'm tired. It's been a long day and I've had too much champagne.'

The Painter held up the other half of the sandwich. 'Do you want this?'

Emily dropped her head onto the table top and shook it.

The Painter quietly munched his way through the second half of the sandwich and drank the water with it. The frothy bubbles swilled the lifeless meal over his tongue and around his cheeks. There was no flavour to impregnate his receptors with taste. He left the crust in the plastic carton and threw the empty water bottle in the bin. Then he too rested his head on the top of the desk. It felt cool and pleasant, in opposition to the growing discomfort of his now expanded stomach. He breathed out across its white surface and watched with one eye open as the moisture gathered and then dispersed immediately.

Emily finally propped her head back up. She watched The Painter's head as he rolled it back and forth along her desk top. 'Christ, what a fucking day. Look at us, we should be celebrating. You sold a painting for a substantial sum of money and I get a nice cut from the sale.'

The Painter looked up, puzzled, half remembering a conversation about the sale. 'Who bought the painting?'

Emily stood up, stretched in an attempt to freshen herself. 'What?' she asked lazily.

'The painting. You said I sold a painting. Who bought it?'

'What does it matter?'

'I don't know.' But The Painter knew it was meant to matter.

'The buyer was anonymous,' she shrugged. 'It happens sometimes. It was purchased through a third party. It was a trusted source, so you don't have to worry, you'll get your money.'

'Money?'

Emily smiled. 'Oh, I forgot you artists don't worry about anything as vulgar as money. Well, it'll keep your soul in food and wine for the time being.'

'My soul?'

She shrugged again. 'Your integrity if you prefer, then.'

'I'd prefer the painting.'

'Really? Well you can always knock another one out easily enough.'

'Can I?'

'You're not starting to doubt your own genius, are you? Don't let any of the people downstairs hear you. They wouldn't feel kindly disposed towards a depreciation in their investment.'

The Painter said nothing and instead began to wheel himself around in Emily's office chair. He gripped hold of the edge of the desk and spun himself around. When he came to stop he did the same thing again.

He half-closed his eyes and watched the box files become a grey mass. The sketches for the gallery exhibition, pinned up on the far wall, became a squiggly mess. The magazines whizzed past in a muddy sludge constructed of both bright and dull colours. He finally came to an abrupt stop when Emily's hands pinned the arms of the chair securely rigid.

'I think we're finished here, don't you? Let's get out of this place before you break my chair and I have to spend tomorrow sitting on the floor.'

Emily moved across the office to the door and held it open for The Painter. He stood with a wobble and began to make his way circuitously around her desk, pressing down on it with his left hand. He used the central table as a prop while making his way to the door. Emily waited patiently for him to reach her. He stopped and met her face-to-face. Hers was a beautiful and flawless face. The most perfect thing he had ever seen. There didn't appear to be a crease or a blemish; just a smooth, symmetrical apparition. The Painter raised his right hand and held it sideways-on to Emily's face, splitting her features straight down the middle. He moved his head from one side to the other. There appeared to be little difference from left to right. There was a simplicity and a purity to the vision and he couldn't tear his eyes from it. Emily remained motionless, not even blinking, before puckering her lips slightly and scowling. The Painter was entranced. Her face seemed to exist in an unchallengeable, perfect form. It was an essence so inescapably sublime, he couldn't possibly capture such a thing.

'Do you want to take a picture?' Emily joked and finally broke the spell.

'No.' The Painter answered resolutely, turning for the doorway. Emily remained for a moment, staring at the wall, before glancing disconsolately around the office. She closed the door silently and then made her way along the corridor on The Painter's trail.

At the top of the stairway they could hear that the noise in the gallery below had subdued from earlier. They both descended to the ground floor in a coupling of inertia. They neither spoke nor looked at one another.

When they had reached the bottom of the stairs they turned left and walked into the first gallery space. The previous crowd had reduced significantly from before. There remained several small groups interlocked in discussion; none were viewing the artworks.

The Painter and Emily moved rapidly through the large room, not engaging with anyone else. In one corner of the space, Francesca was having a téte-a-téte with Urs. She waved mildly at Emily, who nodded back.

In the reception area of the gallery, the doorman remained on duty. Emily passed him by with a quiet goodnight and he replied in kind. The Painter said nothing as he and Emily exited the building.

The street was dark but no less elegant. Shop lights still buzzed and flags still fluttered. The restaurant on the corner was doused in fairy lights. Across the street walked a silver-haired gentleman in a long grey woollen coat. Gracing his flank was an attractive elderly woman resplendent in a mid-length black mink coat.

Emily had no trouble flagging down a taxi. The driver stopped right beside her on the kerb. She opened the door and entered, before beckoning The Painter inside. He climbed into the cab and before he could even sit down, they were clattering off. He collapsed briefly onto Emily's lap before being nudged over to his side.

'Nice night?' the driver enquired.

'Not really,' Emily snapped back.

'Champagne and sandwiches,' The Painter spluttered out.

'Sounds like my kind of shindig.' The driver laughed.

'You weren't babysitting,' Emily muttered, unclear as to who she was addressing.

The Painter leaned his head back and closed his eyes. He listened to the slick of the tyres rolling along the tarmac. They had a soporific effect on him. The swish became a whoosh, which translated into a hush. The wheels in his mind kept on trundling into the night. Long into some unrealised fixed point on the horizon. He tried to adjust his breathing to bring it in line with the sounds of other cars passing by, but the frequency was too fragmented.

The Painter felt a hand touch his. It was smooth with some minor wrinkles. He caught some wisps of a gentle sobbing. His eyes remained shut: his breathing unregulated. He envisioned that face, that preposterously beautiful face, with tears rolling across it, washing that untarnished skin translucent. 'Emily.' He mouthed the word silently to himself. She was beyond a name, beyond a past, and beyond a future. She existed only in the corporeal now. An untainted image of physical perfection.

The taxi glided to a standstill. The Painter opened his eyes, looked out of the cab window, and stared at the door of his building. 'Are we here?' he asked.

'Well, I'm not taking you to my place,' Emily sniffed. 'For one thing, you're not housetrained.'

The driver glanced back and smiled. Emily coldly passed him some money. The tip was big enough to keep the smile on his face.

The Painter managed to extricate himself from the taxi with the minimum amount of fuss. Emily swiftly followed. She slammed the door of the taxi hard and the car drifted off softly into the night.

'That fucking driver never took his eyes off me the whole time. Did you see him?' she entreated The Painter.

'I had my eyes closed.'

'Typical.' Emily marched up the front steps of the building. The Painter duly followed and stood by the front door with her, as though waiting to be invited in.

'Haven't you got your keys?' she asked impatiently, before fetching a set from her bag. She guessed the correct key first time and went straight inside.

The building felt dark and gloomy. A contrast to the bright lights and gaiety of the street they had just come from. The Painter glanced backwards to watch a burly man across the street toss half an animal carcass onto his shoulder. The head and feet had been removed, the innards eviscerated. He wondered what kind of mammal it had once been. The flesh seemed oddly drained of composition under the dull streetlights. It appeared scrubbed and bleached: shorn of any waking resemblance to farmyard fodder.

Emily too was standing watching the nightly procession across the road from The Painter's studio building.

'Is that why you picked this place?' she asked.

'This place?'

'Because of the meat-market. All of those butchers with their rows of gory feasts. All reds and pinks and browns. All that splenetic rage and violence rendered palatable. Like your paintings.'

'My paintings?'

'It's a good spot, a clever spot for such a visceral artist.' Emily began to climb the stairs.

The Painter moved lumberingly behind her.

'I couldn't live with it,' Emily continued. 'All that coming and going at all hours of the night with dead animals. I noticed when we were getting out of the taxi that the smell drifts over the street. The lingering stench of death. I wouldn't like to live in such close proximity to it. Animals that have had their throats slit, the blood drained from them. Perhaps I should become a vegetarian. I would if I had to live here.' She had reached the door to The Painter's studio. She took out the keys again and unlocked it.

Once inside the space, they stood side by side in silence. There was a minimal orange glow emanating from the streetlights outside. It was warm in the room and the smell of oil paints felt mildly repulsive. The various thinners added to a feeling of oppressiveness. Emily made to switch on the light but The Painter arrested her hand.

'No,' he said firmly, before moving through to the living area.

As Emily entered the room and closed the door to the studio, she noticed The Painter sitting in the dark, on the sofa, his eyes closed. He wore a disgruntled expression; the air of a man exasperated with the world. She placed the keys on the kitchen island and glanced back towards the door which led to the studio. She passed the keys through her fingers and back into her bag, adding her gloves a moment later, after she had peeled them off.

Emily switched on the lights to illuminate the kitchen area of the room and headed for the coffee machine. In the fridge she found a tin of Illy freshly-ground coffee. She unscrewed the top and breathed deeply inside. The strong, grainy, bitter waft caught her nose and mouth. She perked up immediately and headed towards the coffee machine, inserting the larger double espresso filter into the detachable handle and switching on the machine as she filled the filter with coffee, before refitting the handle. Emily took a white cup and saucer from nearby and placed the cup on top of the grille underneath the handle. When the light turned green, she pressed a button and the coffee began to slowly drain into the cup. As the cup filled to three-quarters-full she turned off the machine and allowed the crema to swarm around the top. She placed the cup upon the saucer and picked it up in her left hand.

Emily held the warm coffee under her nose, as the smoky bitterness wafted around the room. She sighed a little to herself as she took her first sip. It had been hours since her last cup. It was a small victory to end the day: a late evening cup of coffee. The deep flavour ruminated around her palette. It gave a dark, deep coating to her mouth. A sweeping of cocoa, spicy barbecue, and heavy cigar tobacco. A rich, smooth, leathery taste. She searched around in the fridge for some chocolate to compliment it, but could find none.

The imprint of her lipstick remained on the rim of the cup. Emily looked at its ragged design and made another mark deliberately, further round the edge. The warm, strong, black, frothy liquid contrasted with the clean, pure white of the cup. She swilled the remaining contents around before sucking them up through her teeth. She made her way to the sink and sprayed the coffee from her mouth around its surface. She dropped the cup into the sink and it cracked. Emily pulled the cracked handle off and pressed it into her left thumb. She squeezed until it drew a spot of blood. She ran her bleeding thumb along her teeth. It squealed against the enamel and she pulled it from her mouth. Her nail varnish remained perfectly intact.

Emily opened her bag and took out a small black compact with a design of two interlocking Cs on the front. She opened it and stared at the mirror. There was no blood on her teeth: no coffee stains on her lips. She looked at her eyes, which appeared strained and sleepy. Her skin looked blotchy; she pinched it a little to try and add a more uniform colour. She hadn't drunk as much water as she normally would have and she had consumed two glasses of champagne, several canapés, and an illicit late-night cup of coffee. She had also missed her Monday night session at the gym, which she would have followed with a leisurely swim and a pore-cleansing stretch in the sauna.

The compact snapped tight as Emily watched The Painter sleeping. She walked over to the seating area, unfurled her coat, and threw it over a chair. The Painter was seated with his head tilted back, a trickle of saliva running down his chin. He had the appearance of a drunk who had been hit by a car on the way home from a bar and who would awake in the morning to the drumroll of the mother and father of all hangovers.

Emily put her face close to The Painter's. The smell from him was a toxic mix of aftershave, alcohol, urine, vomit, and, incongruously, a hint of mayonnaise. She stepped backwards and stared at him: the great painter. The artist that she had given up art because of. The artist that caused the end of her most important relationship. There he was, sitting before her, snoring and drooling on a sofa.

'Cunt.' The word filled the silence of the room and created its own void: a lack of appeasement with her younger self. A man she revered and reviled in equal measure lay collapsed in an exhausted state of unconsciousness. What would the younger Emily have done? To be in his orbit, an inner member of his circle, and not some silly little art student confined to living in his shadow. She wanted to kick him hard in the face. Tear her nails into his skin. Bite and slap him until he suffered a great, aching pain. A pain as great as somebody ripping his heart out, through the ribcage, and devouring it there and then. She wanted him to know and acknowledge that the direction her life had taken was all his fault.

She moved forward, picked up his right arm, and pulled it up and over her shoulder and neck. The Painter stirred and briefly opened his half-dead eyes, before closing them again. Emily hauled him into an upright position and began the slog towards the bed. His feet shuffled along unwillingly and his head swung from one side to another.

When Emily had reached the bed, she slung The Painter down on top of it. 'I don't get paid enough,' she told his inert form as she panted above it.

She cautiously undressed him: first the shoes, then the socks, which she tossed onto the floor by the bed. Next she wrestled him out of his jacket and threw it across the room. She peeled his t-shirt up over his head, raised it to her face, and smelled it. The cotton was freshly laundered, but nevertheless had a stale quality to it. She looked down. The Painter's torso was lean but not toned. He had a rough patch of dark hair in the centre of his chest, though the rest was relatively smooth.

Emily unbuttoned his trousers and pulled them down. She gathered them up in a heap, careful not to disturb the contents of the pockets. Underneath were a pair of black Calvin Klein shorts. She baulked at touching them and sat pensively on the side of the bed.

She caught the words 'I love you'. She turned to The Painter in shock. He was breathing heavily with his eyes closed. The voice was unfamiliar but it resonated from a long time ago. She saw a young man lying on the bed with her; naked, smiling. He hadn't been the first, but he was the one she had wanted. The first one she fell in love with; the only one she fell in love with. She had slept with some since, but it didn't mean the same. It was a physical desire and nothing more. They all left her so cold; as cold as that boy on the slab, the one they would never let her see. One last moment to say goodbye, to say sorry.

The Painter struggled into her vision. 'Emily, you're so

beautiful; so perfect.' She looked towards him and realised he was in a state of excitement. With trepidation, she grappled with The Painter's shorts. They felt faintly damp and as she held them close she could smell the urine. She threw them as far across the room as she could.

There he was, the great painter, half-conscious, naked and erect on his bed. Emily picked up a pillow from the floor and tossed it over his face. She looked his body over. It was not that of a young man. It was showing wear and tear. There was a scar running several centimetres up the right shin.

She hadn't seen a young man's body since back then. She couldn't bear it. She preferred the older men, who didn't remind her of him.

She touched The Painter's feet: stroked along them. Wondering how cold the boy on the slab must have been. The legs and chest in front of her were mildly tanned and warm to the touch. His would have been withered and mottled grey. He'd had a beautiful face; all the girls thought so. He hadn't been wearing his seatbelt. What would that windscreen have done to that face? When had she last seen him? What were the words she used? When had the last time been? When they were happy together. With each other, alone in the universe.

Emily asked The Painter, 'Do you have anything?'

'What?' came the garbled, incomprehensive reply.

She lifted the pillow. 'Protection?'

'I don't know.'

Emily opened the top drawer of the cabinet next to his bed. There was a wooden cigar box. She took it out and felt along its smooth surface before smelling its grain. Inside the box were red-wrapped Durex condoms. She retrieved one and replaced the box in the drawer.

Slowly, she unlaced her boots and kicked them off. Then she pulled down her tights and dropped them on the floor, followed by her knickers. She ripped open the condom packet and took the coiled latex parcel out.

The Painter lay still; his eyes half-open and staring at Emily. The pillow was leaning upright on top of his forehead. She checked which way the condom rolled out, before teasing it over The Painter's penis.

Once in place, Emily straddled The Painter and, putting her hand beneath her dress, guided him into her. She started to move up and down in a slow, rhythmic movement. The Painter stared up at her, his eyes now fully awake. She dropped the cushion down over his face once more.

Her mind returned to the boy. She hadn't been his first either, but she had been his best. She knew he had improved with her. He had trusted her and told her things. She had taught him not to feel ashamed. That it was just them, that it was fun, and that it was an expression of love. He was more timid than her, alone, in the bedroom. There was a kind of sweetness and chivalry to him. Her friends all found it endearing. Some hardly spoke to her after the break-up. Then after his death she became persona non grata. She didn't know why she had stayed at university. Perhaps to be near him. As if it hadn't happened.

None of it was real. He wasn't on that slab anymore. He was in a grave, in a small churchyard, in his home town. By now he would have been through putrefaction and become withered skin and protruding bones. The flesh was dead, the heart was dead, and the spirit was dead. It was all dead and she had killed it. And he had helped her do it.

Emily began shaking with emotion as she pressed down harder and harder on The Painter. Tears streamed from her eyes and her nose began to dribble into her mouth. She started to cry loudly and she punched out at the pillow still covering The Painter's face. She punched it and punched it again and again. There was a groaning from underneath it and Emily stopped suddenly. She quickly clambered from The Painter and collapsed onto the floor, crying hysterically.

The Painter peeled the pillow from his face. His left eye was swelling and he had a gash in his eyebrow which was leaking blood into his eye. He staggered his way into an upright position and looked down at the condom, which was sitting halfway off his deflating penis. He pulled at the thin latex skin and snapped it free. He held the fatter, unrolled, end between his forefinger and thumb and dangled the condom in front of his face. The teat end contained an amount of milky fluid. He shook the condom lightly from side-to-side, before drooping it cautiously into his mouth. It tasted of a synthetic, mildly salty, strawberry flavour. He pushed his teeth together at the teat and moved the fluid around a little. The sensation was an amalgam of the organic and the chemical. He let the condom enter his mouth towards the throat, at which point he began to gag and made to vomit. He immediately pulled the condom from his mouth as a second revulsive reflex brought some vomit into his throat. He gagged and then swallowed the residue of acrid sickness. He took the condom and threw it over towards the corridor leading to the bathroom.

Emily was seated on the floor with her face in her hands. Her shoulders rocked mildly as she continued sobbing.

'Sorry,' The Painter offered meekly.

She turned towards him, her face streamed with tears and mascara. She examined his face and the blood trickling down over his left eye and onto his cheek. 'Oh God! What have I done!' She began to cry more deeply.

'It's okay,' The Painter exclaimed as he rubbed blood away with the back of his right hand. He took the blood and wiped it on the wall next to him in a calm, circular motion. Then he gripped the pillow and felt along the blood stain smeared into the cotton fibres. He smelled at the stale cloth and the earthy, metallic, scarlet slick.

He looked at the back of Emily's head shaking convulsively. Her red hair was still perfectly coiffured, her shoulders narrow, her arms slender. The light peach skin looked smooth along her left arm. There was a blemish part-way down, of indented scarred tissue, the result of an adolescent inoculation. The Painter leaned over and touched the aberration on the otherwise flawless surface. A little circle of imperfection taunting the perception of the wholesome, unfettered domination of sublime beauty.

She turned to look at him, her eyes filled with horror and remorse. He slumped back down on the bed.

'I don't know what happened. I lost control. I'm really sorry. I'm under a lot of stress at the moment. I've got a lot of pressures in my private life. I'm seeing somebody. Somebody I shouldn't be seeing. It's complicated,' she shrugged. 'But today, I keep on thinking about that old love affair. About that boy who died, and how I killed him and how much I still miss him and want him. You can understand, can't you? I mean, you must have been in a situation like that at least once in your life. Perhaps when you were younger.' Emily looked up at The Painter expectantly but there was no reply. 'I need to fix that eye, maybe you need to go to hospital with it.' She finally composed herself enough to get up off the floor. The Painter lay still on the bed, his eyes closed, snoring. 'It was all so innocent back then,' she told his inert form.

CHAPTER 12

The thudding in his head brought The Painter into consciousness. It felt like an endless series of sliding punches. His right eye opened limply, but his left remained resolutely shut. It felt as though it had ballooned up in the night. He pushed at it with his hand. The nerve-endings viciously defended themselves with a shock to his brain that brought a piercing scream into the front of his head, down through his jaw and teeth, and into his neck. The tension was broken by channelling the pain into a loud, invigorating howl of agony.

He took his right fist and buried it hard into the mattress, through which he proceeded to repeatedly try to punch a hole. The mattress dented briefly but swiftly sprung back to its uniform shape. The Painter lodged his left index finger against his left nostril and pressed hard. Through his right nostril, he violently blew out a rash of mucus, which dripped stalagmite-like towards the bed. He swiped his right hand across his nose to detach the thick, gloopy thread, smearing it across the crusty, blood-stained sheet in revenge.

The Painter scanned the room. It was as before: everything out of place. A living quarters decorated by spit and semen; blood and urine; vomit and excrement. The room stank of a kind of wilful decay. The walls and ceiling and floor felt heavier every day. As though the weight of substances would finally defeat them and they would collapse within themselves and field a giant, soiled void instead. An intensely rancid, sulphurous cesspool of a putrid brown hue. He listlessly awaited that moment when the room would drag him too into its detritus-ridden vortex.

The room remained passively neutral. The sunlight cut through the space, highlighting a billowing stream of dust filled with hair and skin tissue. It trapped them in its projected rays as they danced their way through the seated area and kitchen.

The Painter stretched out a trembling arm to grasp them. His stomach rumbled briefly before seizing him more violently. In response, he stumbled from the bed and moved towards the kitchen. On the way, he attempted to devour some of the dust particles. With his mouth agape, he trawled past the armchair and around the kitchen island. He could not conceive of any sense of taste or nourishment being provided.

The lights on the coffee machine were turned on, red and green. There was a slightly charred smell in the air. The Painter detached the filter holder. Inside was a dried-out clump of black coffee. He instinctively pushed in his tongue and immediately recoiled at the burning sting inflicted on its tip. He gripped the holder under his chin and ejected a long, foaming drizzle of spit into the charred remnants of the used grains. He struck the filter with the end of his tongue and once more it stung, the granules remaining immovable. Finally, he simply ejected the filter from the handle into the sink and switched the machine off at the socket. The Painter turned on the red tap and aimed the rush of water at the filter. He took the thumb of his right hand and began to massage the coffee grains loose. The coffee began to spurt out over the sink and onto the skin of his hand. He looked down at the deep brown flecks infecting his flesh and began to suck them into his mouth. He tasted the mildly bitter tang of overcooked coffee and spat the tiny, blackened lumps back into the sink.

The creases and convulsions in his gut continued to harangue The Painter. He opened one of the kitchen cupboards and felt inside. There was a half-eaten loaf of bread, which he pulled out and lay on the kitchen worktop. Taking the first slice of bread from its plastic wrapping, he held it aloft. There were blue-green spores stretched across it, in a dark ploy to sprout some kind of fungal infection within the dry wheat fibres. He bit into the slice and spat it back out immediately. The stale, mildew flavour activated a mild retching of his stomach and he began to suffer dart-like stabbing pains. He pushed the loaf of bread onto the floor and began to scavenge again in the cupboard. Inside, he discovered a jar filled with a brown chocolate paste, topped with a large white lid. He wheeled the lid from the jar and inhaled the nutty, sweet autumnal smell that greeted him. He stuck two fingers deep into the jar and pulled out a portion of the sticky, smooth paste from inside. The offending fingers were plunged straight away into The Painter's mouth. He masticated the chocolate paste around his teeth and tongue, devouring its dryly sweet flavour. He continued to scour three fingers around the jar and back into his ravaged mouth until he had expended the contents of the pot. He sucked and licked at his fingers until all they retained were the tacky remnants of his sticky saliva.

The Painter suddenly became all too aware of his desperate need to use the toilet. His erect penis bulged with urine and the urgency to piss was too great to attempt any further movement. He gripped the hard-on in his hands, stood on his tiptoes, and began to urinate in the sink. The golden liquid sprayed over the far side, over the taps, and onto the wall. He couldn't control its flow or its dispersal. In a splaying arc, it hit several places at once. When he eventually stopped, the streaming sunlight glistened over the kitchen surfaces now infected with its newly-released ammonium dew.

With his penis still grasped firmly in his right hand, The Painter raised his left hand up to his left eye. He could feel along the thinly crisped-over scab on his eyelid. His tear ducts smarted as he pressed in gently. A smidgeon of bloody residue escaped onto his finger. He took it and drew a line down the centre of his cock with it.

He looked around the living area and bedroom for

Emily. There was no trace of her. He walked back to the bed, searching the living room furniture on the way for leftover garments but he could find none. The bedroom floor was Emily-free, as was the actual bed.

The Painter kneeled down on the hard, dark parquet blocks that made up the flooring and sniffed along the bedsheets in a desire for her elusive fragrance. He ran his nostrils around and over a large surface of the mattress, but the hints of her allure were so distant as to be insufficiently recognisable. The only thing he could truly detect was an ingrained earthiness of sweat, dribble, puke, and shit marks, within a severe state of fevered decomposition. Emily was gone: her presence had evaporated.

A crumpled sheet had been cast on the floor as well as a suit jacket, trousers, t-shirt, shorts and socks. The Painter slumped down beside them. He took the sheet and rubbed it between his fingers. He sniffed at it in vain. The space was empty of all but him.

When had she left? Had she been there at all? The red hair, the beautiful face, the blemish-free skin. The room held no memory of her. Emily had disappeared. She may never have existed. A fantasy he had spun himself.

The Painter started to crawl along the floor, sniffing at the scarred, tightly woven wood. It had an ethereal smell of nature, with a dusty fatigue. There were no real scents captured among its protective grains. He felt along it with his hands, seeking out the random markings of Emily's heels. Some spiked grooves dug into almost imperceptible edges. He looked for her boots, her stockings, her knickers, but all in vain.

The flooring by the door was still moist and sticky. He could smell the trace of urine from the day before. He stood up and gripped hold of the radiator. It was still hot and he retracted his already injured hand with a yelp.

Could he search her out? The ghost called Emily. He didn't know the location of the gallery she worked in. He remembered she had a key. Would she return?

The Painter moved through to the bathroom. A sickly stench of aftershave resolutely permeated the air. He walked to the sink and stared at the shards of the broken blue bottle from the day before then felt along the cool tiles and stepped under the shower. On the wall were some faint pink marks running down the grouting. He turned the water on, tensing his whole body against the sharp blast, which forced him to move backwards quickly and knock the back of his head against the wall. For a split second his vision went blank, before a wild throbbing started. The pain at the back of his head was in counterpoint to that which still beat at his frontal lobes.

The steam rose up out of the stream of water and The Painter plunged himself under it with a strained caution. His hair started to dampen, then soak, and the water began to wash down his body. He looked upwards and attempted to open his left eye. His efforts proved fruitless: it was locked tight. Some blood started to release itself from his wound and trickle over his body towards the plughole. Carrying on down into the sewers, bringing a part of him to the foundations of the city. The animals in the meat-market, their blood slowly being swept away to co-mingle with his in an abattoir's dance of death.

He picked up a plastic bottle on the floor and squeezed some of the creamy contents into his palm. It had a fresh, zesty fragrance with a floral hint. He rubbed the liquid all over his body, into his face and over his hair. The cleansing lotion bubbled up and caressed his open pores. They were clearing out and washing away all the filth and iniquities, the bodily fluids; the sweat and blood and urine and excrement and vomit and skin. Funnelling it all towards the city's underbelly to merge with the dirt and grime and sewage. To be swilled around in the vagrant company of the city's underground denizens, whose army was made up of rats and mice and lice and fleas and bugs and insects and other brands of vermin. Everything flowed towards the muddy, cavernous waters of the river and from there out into the glowing expanse of the great blue ocean.

'You are formed of substance and substance dissipates.' The words appeared to come from the showerhead. The Painter gazed up at the flow of water cascading towards him, drenching his skin. The final streaks of soap slurped down through the plughole as The Painter turned off the shower.

He moved over to the mirror and gazed at his bulbous left eye, with its swirling spread of purple and black. On his eyebrow was a small, raw gash with a ripped scab and festering blood. The Painter took hold of the thin slither of skin covering the wound and yanked it away from its knotting sinew. He held it in his fingers. It was a slim piece of encrusted blood. He pushed it up into his right nostril, where it jabbed at the sensitive inner membrane. This caused a sharp intake of breath through his teeth, before he pulled the scab back down. He examined it with his one good eye. A dehydrated piece of flotsam torn from his face: connective tissue now dead in his hand. He threw it into his mouth and chomped down on the crispy flesh. He tasted nothing and felt nothing.

The Painter turned from his reflected form and trudged his way back through to the bedroom. His damp feet were slippery on the floor and as he entered the doorway he slithered slightly before grasping for the doorpost. As he steadied himself, he noticed something on the floor. A piece of discarded rubbish clumped down on the dense wood finish. He scrambled onto his knees and moved towards the vagrant matter. Picking it up tweezer-like in the fingers of his right hand, he examined the soiled condom. There was a piece of light fluff and a black curly hair attached to it and it was smudged inside with a milky fluid. Was this evidence of Emily: of her presence? The missing part of a puzzle?

He willed into form the slim, long legs, the sleek monochrome dress, the bobbing red hair, the large green eyes, the dark smoky lashes, the pouting lips, the smooth pink skin, the boots pinched tight against the ankles, the black stockings, the long silk gloves, pulling the condom over his hard penis, working it down, straddling him and pushing him all the way inside, cocooned in her flesh, pulling back and forth, his face smothered, grasping for breath, the crying, the cold, hard punching, the arse tightening, the capillaries opening, the muscles contracting, the semen spurting.

The Painter groaned as his hand gently came to a rest. He looked down at the half-pulled-on condom, wrinkled and emaciated and spattered with sperm. He stood still and put his hands up to his eyes. They began to well up with tears. He gripped his fists together against his eyeballs as the dangling condom slipped off his deflating penis and fell to the floor. His connection to Emily was gone again. He couldn't hold on to her arms, feel her breasts against his chest, hear her breath against his ear. He felt down along his nipples and grasped at his chest hair, gripping and tearing at his sparse thatch.

The room began to feel unattached as it rattled and wobbled underneath The Painter's feet. He kept his right eye closed and moved forwards, left arm outstretched, until he reached the bookshelf. He felt along the books' hard spines and eventually gripped hold of one for ballast. The book fell out of the shelf and into his waiting arms. He looked down at the cover, its title *Albrecht Dürer: The Complete Oeuvre*. The coverline had been written over a picture of a long-haired, long-faced, bearded man with a penetrating stare. A searing portrait of an enigmatic figure, both benevolent and malevolent: part Christ and part Rasputin. The tendrils of his hair had the slight appearance of chains and his face was as intelligent as it was melancholic. There was an arrogance apparent in the portrait juxtaposed with a certain vulnerability.

The Painter moved his right hand across the figure. He felt the smooth sheen of the book's dust cover. He opened the book and flicked through its pages. A pair of blue praying hands whirled past and a naked man and woman, then some black-and-white prints. He smelled the pages with their glossy, earthy imprimatur, and then held the book firmly to his chest. After holding the volume for a moment, he let it slide out of his hands and fall to the floor. The hard-edged corner hit two of The Painter's toes before landing on the ground. He immediately crippled over and screamed out. He felt with his hands towards his feet and noted an indented mark on one toe and a cut on the other.

He gripped the foot in his left hand and squeezed hard, then rubbed both toes as he hobbled towards the cabinet in which his clothes were held. He sat on the floor, destitute and disturbed, staring up at the cold, metallic piece of office furniture. His body felt as gnarled as the hands in the Dürer picture; it was filled with cuts and grazes and bruises and wounds and gashes and slashes and scabs and was washed and doused in the colours of pink and red and blue and purple and black. He ached in every part of his anatomy. His toes and shins were battered, his cock was dry and limp, his hands were cut and beaten, his chest was scratched and scrawled, and his face and head were busted and broken. A ragged stretch of ripped and torn flesh held aloft by a weary skeleton.

He touched the cold, grey metal drawers and pulled one open at random. He took from it a pair of black woollen socks. He rubbed the soft texture over his body as though it might have some talismanic healing powers, before peeling the socks apart and pulling one over his right foot. The damaged toes on his left foot throbbed slightly, though the pain had subsided as he peeled the remaining sock over it, wincing. He pulled open the next drawer and took from it a pair of black Calvin Klein shorts which had a white logo-rich band around the top. From the next drawer, he retrieved a white t-shirt, which he began to pull over his head and roll down his chest.

The Painter scrambled over the floor towards his dishevelled garments from the evening before. He picked out the trousers, wound them over his legs, and attached them around his waist. He took the jacket and threw it over his shoulders, stretching it over his arms. Next came the black leather shoes, which he slipped onto his feet by shoe-horning the soft leather at the heels with his fingers.

Dressed, he scoured the room with his one undamaged eye. It looked as obliterated as his body felt. He gripped hold of the mattress, dragged himself upright, and began to wander the space. He couldn't feel any essence of Emily. Her presence was entirely lost to him.

He slid his hand into his pocket and pulled out the unfamiliar mobile phone that still resided there. He pushed the bottom and the screen lit up. A text message had been sent by Dan Smithson, giving the location of The Siberian. The message also implored The Painter to seek the money-lender out and to negotiate, 'an equitable deal'.

The Painter had no idea what that might mean. Dan Smithson had spoken to him already about this matter, but he was entirely unclear as to what his exact role was. He sensed that he was expected to be some kind of intermediary between the two men. How was he to pay The Siberian money for Dan Smithson? He hadn't yet collected the money from the sale of his paintings.

He put the phone in his pocket and sat down carefully on the soiled mattress, opening the top drawer in his bedside cabinet. Inside there was the wooden cigar box, which he took out and opened. There were around half-a-dozen condoms left inside. He picked one up and felt its smooth, shiny surface. He smelled it but struggled to find a trace of strawberry. He packed the condom back into the box and placed it back in the drawer, which he closed. He moved one drawer down and pulled it open. Sitting inside was a lone pile of bank notes, of various denominations. He pulled the fat wad out and fanned the notes through his hands. He held them to his nose and sniffed at them. They smelled inky and sterile, machine-pressed slithers of paper, printed on and passed through hand to hand. Some were grubbier than others, but they appeared remarkably impervious to their commercial peregrinations. They had not absorbed anything of the world onto their imprint.

The Painter stuffed the money into the front pocket of his suit jacket, gathered himself up wearily, and made his way through the debris of his living quarters.

Inside the studio, the light was streaming in. It bounced off the blank white canvases stacked together against the wall. They reflected the light into the room, warming it with an enticing glow. The Painter picked up a wooden brush and ruffled its soft horsehairs. The brush was clean and unused. He rubbed it along his cheeks, before tickling himself with it under the chin. He brushed it along the backs of his hands and across the deep gash which wept into the hairs of his left hand. He took the brush and scumbled it across the already soiled, slashed canvas. The mark it left was indecipherable. He layered the brush with a long gob of spit and rubbed it into the cotton weave. It merely left a mild, nondescript stain. The Painter punched the canvas instead, ramming the brush clean through its now ruptured surface and into the wall. He left the brush positioned there. Then he leaned his head against the canvas and rubbed his left cheek along the smooth material. The Painter pressed his tongue out and into the white cotton and began to lick. Its texture was rougher on the tongue than it had been on his skin. It was dull and tasteless, with a minor measure of a glutinous resin.

He eventually turned from the canvas and exited the studio, into the corridor. He started to descend the stairs. His legs felt weak at the exertion and he contemplated whether there could be an eatery close by. The chocolate spread had merely served to goad his stomach on to further greed. The Painter found himself stealthily crafting his way to the bottom of the staircase by clinging on to the wooden banister. His shoes clumped their way over the shiny flooring to the front door.

Once outside, the sun was shining gloriously and it was tolerably pleasant but for a chilly breeze. The market across the road was now simply humming with labour; a few vans came and went, but there were no burly men hanging carcasses on their backs. The Porsche sat gleaming in the sunlight, as it bounced off the racing-green exterior and lit up the grubby, grey street. The Painter looked up and down the road for a food shop, but there appeared to be none. He walked over and unlocked the door to the Porsche. On the windscreen he saw another plastic yellow packet. He peeled it off and regarded it momentarily before tossing it aside. He felt the smooth, clean lines of the car, its metal warmed slightly under the gentle gaze of the sun. The paintwork seemed impervious to harm despite the deep grooves he had gored into it earlier and he fought an urge to continue his excoriating decoration, forever damaging what was the perfect embodiment of a clinical coating for a machine-manufactured, precision piece of metal. He drew his nails across it, but they could not penetrate its powerful sheen.

Inside the car, the stitched leatherwork was warming and extruding a scent of finely-crafted animal hide, washed and purged and upholstered for the mechanical age, which couldn't be more different from the carcasses that passed it in the night. The Painter eased himself behind the wheel and squeezed himself in against the comfortable seating. He turned the key and worked over the engine, which hummed into power. He input The Siberian's address into the satellite navigation system and pulled out into the street.

The mild grubbiness and sleaze of his milieu began to swiftly transform into something less angularly urban. There were men in pinstriped suits and women in dark and sombre attire. Brash and bold streets began to develop and a few skyscrapers started to enter into his focus. The Painter's stomach ached violently and his vision was tiring. The left eye remained violently enclosed and the right was wavering into unconsciousness. He turned into a wide, soberly busy street in which a silver bubble-like structure was parked. People were walking away from it with food in their hands. He pulled in and parked the Porsche directly in front of the mobile stand. The vehicle hit the kerb first with the front wheel and then the back. A man in a long black coat and dark suit turned fractiously towards the car and scowled aggressively at The Painter, who switched off the car engine and opened the door into the street.

Upon stepping out of the car, a van flashed past within a hair's whisper of him and the occupant flung out, 'Fucking dick!' as he passed. The Painter glanced curiously after him then closed the car door and walked over to the pavement.

The queue in front of the food stand had thinned. There was a woman in a cream Mackintosh that covered a black jacket and skirt, paired with sensible black shoes. She took her closed, clear plastic carton filled with salad and her fruit smoothie and walked back towards a nondescript office block made of a vast curtain of glass. The man in front of The Painter was dressed in a slim dark grey suit, with a purple shirt and a pink tie. He had thick brown hair which had been swept back off his forehead with product. The man ordered falafels in pitta bread with salad and chillies, and a bottle of sparkling mineral water on the side. The Painter watched the food vendor fill the flatbread with salad, followed by small, round, fried brown balls, before drizzling the juice of crushed chillies over the culinary ensemble. When this service transaction was complete, The Painter walked up to the counter.

'What would you like?' The young man with a thin, neat beard and kind blue eyes smiled at him.

'The same as that man.' The Painter pointed towards the spot where the man in the grey suit had previously stood.

'Falafels in pitta with salad and chillies?'

'Yes,' The Painter replied.

'Do you want mineral water too?'

'Okay.'

As the vendor busied himself with the order, The Painter could feel his whole mouth salivate as his stomach contorted itself in raptures of tight convulsions, ready for the feast. The young man placed the clear water bottle with pearlescent blue writing down on the counter and handed him the pitta bread filled with falafels and fresh salad topped with crushed chillies. The Painter held the food and smelled its healthy earthiness. The chillies singed his nasal passage a little.

'The chillies have a good kick,' the young man said, eyeing The Painter, concerned.

'It's okay.'

The vendor smiled in a lopsided manner. 'So this is the part when you give me the money.'

The Painter pulled out a handful of notes. The vendor plucked one out of his proffered hands. 'You financial types sure like to flash it around.' He placed it in the till and gave The Painter a handful of coins. 'Have a nice day,' he smiled one last time.

'And you.' The Painter walked back to the car, clinging defensively to his lunchtime snack.

He placed the bottle of water on the roof of the car as he opened the door. While he held the door open with his knee, he grabbed the bottle and eased himself into the car with his lunch.

The first bite was exquisite: soft middle-eastern spices with chickpeas, garlic, lemon, and fresh crunchy salad in a warm, comforting flat bread. Then he felt the kick of the chillies. They bit into his lips, his tongue, his palette and his throat. He started to choke them back. He grabbed for the water and took a large slug but it simply served to make things worse. The fizz added to the discontent in his mouth. He swallowed his mouthful then, compelled by his stomach and its insane desire for emancipation, he took another giant bite. The Painter ate as fast as he could in an attempt to lessen the effects of the chillies. With every bite the burning became more pronounced. He swigged back the water in an act of desperation, helping to fuel his mouth with an endlessly rolling cacophony of fire. His head began to sweat, bringing forth dribbles of blood from the wound on his eyebrow. The salt running down over his injured eye made the sensation of pain a moveable purgatory.

He started to cough violently, involuntarily expurgating pieces of falafel and lettuce and bread over the steering wheel, the dashboard, and onto the windscreen.

It was the endgame for his lunch as he threw it violently against the passenger window. The salad and falafels scattered everywhere, onto the dashboard and the floor. The pitta bread landed on the passenger seat. A long smear of crushed chillies adorned the passenger window.

The Painter took the remaining contents of the bottle of mineral water and threw it at the stain. The water hit only the passenger door panel, underneath the window, splashing the seat and the gearstick along the way. He gripped the steering wheel with a ferocity and screamed into it, hitting the horn three times. Several people on the street glanced over to see what the commotion was about but swiftly went on their way again, unwilling to become involved.

The Painter turned the engine over and headed out onto

the street. A passing construction truck honked loudly as it passed too closely and tore off the driver's wing mirror. The Painter juddered to a halt and stalled the car in the middle of the road. A couple of drivers behind him quickly made violent use of their own horns. He started the car again and took off faster than he could handle, narrowly missing mounting the kerb and taking out two young office workers, who were holding hands as they meandered along the pavement.

The car weaved its way through wide then narrow congested streets, where vast elevated, concrete, steel and glass financial cathedrals twisted, bent and swooned their way through the stratosphere. The Painter stared upwards as the buildings further constricted his view and weighed down around his increasingly insignificant vehicle. His heart beat painfully and his breathing quickened. People risked collision with his car by rushing out in front of him in suits and raincoats with bags and satchels and briefcases; they all seemed young and in a hurry. There were scatterings of bars and restaurants, newsagents and street food vendors, with the occasional mid-market clothing store thrown in. The streets began to broaden again and the buildings started to fall away. There were fewer suits and more casual clothing. A street market popped up, running the length of a long, narrow street. The traders and their clientele were far more diverse and cosmopolitan than the pedestrians in the previous streets.

CHAPTER 13

The satellite navigation system brought The Painter further into the heart of a more ramshackle, industrial-looking area, filled with workshops and sweatshops and then just shops with bars and grilles over their windows. The car was advised to stop outside a brown-brick, four-storey building with grubby faded 'To Let' signs in the windows of its ground floor. The Painter parked the Porsche by the side of the road immediately outside the front doors of the building. He sat and watched a group of teenagers, bags slung over their slumped shoulders and books and folders in their hands, talk and laugh with each other across the street. One girl hit a boy playfully and she hid behind her friends as he chased around them to capture her.

Further up his side of the street a raggedy-dressed, middle-aged derelict was foraging in a bin. His exertions were to no avail and he turned his attention to the pavement, where he picked up a cigarette butt and examined it meticulously before placing it in his mouth. He made no attempt to light the cigarette, but continued mooching up the street with his hands crossed behind his back and his nose beaking towards the gutter.

The Painter climbed out of the car and burped loudly. A burning sensation passed up through his chest and throat and out into the warming afternoon air. One of the kids from across the street cast a surprised glance at his rude behaviour and then shouted across 'Nice motor!' before returning to his conversation. The Painter tracked around the car and onto the pavement. He stopped by the front door to the building and bent down to pick up a cigarette stub missed by the earlier forager. It was shorter than the one the tramp had collected and The Painter assumed he had rejected this one on the grounds of its size. He smelled its strong, musty scent before biting into it. He spat it back out immediately as the stale, bitter flavour took root in his mouth. He flicked out errant pieces of tobacco from his lips, using his tongue and then his fingers. A trickle of saliva from the sides of his mouth ran out and down into a crack between the grey, concrete paving stones.

The Painter pushed his way through the heavy wood-and-glass door, into the building. The hallway was filled with a broody, ominous gloom. Shadows from the sunlight outside played along the walls, giving the place a heavy chiaroscuro effect. The corners were masked in darkness, while the metal doors of the lift shone in a greasy, dull silence. The stairs to the side were half-lit in a striking angular cut coming from a high-up window on the façade.

The Painter walked over to the lift and pressed the button. It mechanically clunked into action and began moving down towards him. When it arrived, the doors clattered open in a less than smooth motion, almost sticking half open at one point. Unperturbed, he got in and pressed the button for the fourth floor, as instructed by Dan Smithson in his text. The smell from the lift was a confusing concoction of industrial detergent and stale piss, both of which made The Painter feel nauseated. The lift bumped and ground its way up the floors until it reached its fourth and final destination. The doors opened half-way and then jammed. The Painter stood silently and still until a thick arm pushed the doors aside. A large man, sweating in his shirtsleeves, with a brown kipper tie and a messy tobacco-stained, grey comb-over, stood out from the side of the lift. 'They're always sticking,' he said. 'You just have to give them a good shove.' He held the doors open for The Painter, who cautiously stepped over the threshold of the lift and through the halitosis-ridden breath of the sweating man. He pressed the button marked '4' and rode the clattering contraption until it shuddered to a stop. This time the doors creaked fully open at their first attempt.

Out in the hallway, The Painter glanced up and down the long, gloomy corridor. It was beset with half a dozen doors on either side. He trod along the sticky, green carpet tiles, catching flecks of peeling, yellow paint from the corridor walls, which were so dry and dusty they completely disintegrated in the palm of his hand.

The first door he came to was made of cheap plywood and had no identifying mark on it. The Painter knocked briskly on it but there was no response, even though he could clearly hear footsteps and whispering from inside the room. The next door along, he hit pay dirt. The thick, black print on the rippled glass panel of the wooden door stated it was the place of business of *Emir Costas: Financial Adviser and Accountancy Regulator*. The Painter stared at the lettering and watched intensely as it bent and twisted into a crooked smile. Then the first and second lines appeared to separate and the glass open up to instruct with the words: 'You must negotiate your own invention.' The Painter pushed his hands towards the gaping mouth. He tapped his fingers against the firm substance of the glass panel then ran them along its grooves, the words realigned in their proper order. He pushed his head up to the door and rolled it back and forth, before licking the cool, bumpy surface. He took his right hand and gripped, then turned the cold brass handle and pushed the door inwards.

Once inside, the room was bright and airy, in direct contrast to the corridor outside. It had been whitewashed and its right wall furnished with a couple of black-and-white photographic prints of the ocean, with dolphins and whales leaping from the water. There was a small wooden coffee table with two black leather chairs at either side. To the left of the room was a large wooden desk on which a white desktop computer perched. There was also a red phone and a small white intercom device. Next to the black mouse mat was a pink nail file. To the left side of the desk was a shelving unit filled with box files and folders. To the right there was a square metal unit bearing a printer. The wooden floor of the room had been finely polished and the place exuded the timid smell of a mild air freshener.

In the centre of the back wall was a wooden door which was closed. The Painter stood stock-still in the middle of the office, trying to decide what he should do next, when a female voice from behind him asked, 'Can I help you?'

He turned around to be greeted by a woman in her early thirties, wearing a tight white shirt and a tight black skirt which fell down to just above her knees, with sheer tights and black, patent leather stiletto-heeled shoes. These gave her a greater stature than her small frame commanded. Her shirt was open to the tip of her black bra and she wore a gold chain and crucifix around her neck.

She was an attractive, if unusual-looking, woman, with sharp cheekbones, a sharp chin, and sharp eyes. Her face gave the impression of staring at the pointed blade of a well-crafted spear. Her skin had a soft tan and her thin blonde hair was shoulder-length and cut across her forehead from a side parting. She wore shocking pink lipstick, which perfectly matched the pink polish on her manicured fingernails.

'I'm here to see The Siberian,' The Painter offered confusedly.

'The Siberian?' she replied coldly.

'Yes.'

'Why are you here?'

'Dan Smithson sent me.'

'Wait here,' the woman said irritably as she went through the door at the end of the office, closing it behind her. The Painter watched the door and awaited her return. A few moments passed and she hadn't returned, so he walked over to the door and knocked courteously on it. There was no reply and he opened it for himself.

The second office was longer than the first. There was only one wooden desk, with a brown, leather-backed chair placed in front of it. A green leather blotting pad, a green-

and-gold reading lamp, a thick black ledger, and the same design of intercom as was in the first office, sat on the desk. There was a small, rectangular window on the back wall where wooden Venetian blinds obscured the view. The floor was dominated by a large patterned rug, in a vibrant red, and the wall was hung with a solitary print of a young man crouching in camouflaged fatigues and a black beret, holding a machine gun.

The man himself sat on the other side of the desk, staring malevolently at The Painter as he took in his surroundings. The man wore a light grey shirt with a dark grey tie. His slate-grey suit jacket hung on the back of the chair behind him. His black hair was slicked back to reveal receding sides. He had a wiry build and was tough-looking, the effect slightly offset by a dandyish pencil moustache. He had tight, thin lips and acne scarring on his cheeks. The Painter put his age at early-to-mid-forties.

The woman, seated on the front of the desk, arms folded, stared at The Painter. 'What do you want?'

'To see The Siberian.'

'There is no Siberian.'

The Painter looked around. 'I've got the wrong place.'

'Right place. Wrong person.'

'What?'

'Who sent you?' The man's voice was calm and low, but had a slightly menacing register.

'Dan Smithson.'

'Are you his artist friend, The Painter?'

'The Painter?'

The pair squinted at him, annoyance crossing their faces.

'Sit down,' the man demanded as he waved his hand towards the empty chair.

The Painter walked forwards and sat down. The seat was quite stiff and formal and he attempted to settle himself comfortably.

'Let me tell you something, fella,' the man started. 'My name is Costas and this is my associate, Olga.' He gestured towards the woman, who was still seated on the desk beside The Painter. 'Nobody here is Siberian. I'm Serbian,' he enunciated the word carefully. 'Olga is from the Ukraine. Do you understand?'

'Yes,' The Painter replied.

'Your friend Dan Smithson has imparted some erroneous information to you. There are no Siberians in our organisation. Myself and Olga are living here in exile. We are,' he searched for the correct term, 'refugees, you might say.'

'Refugees?'

'Do you always answer everything with a question?' The Serbian asked with a measure of irritability.

Olga stepped down off the table as Costas leaned forward. 'I don't know what your friend Dan Smithson told you, but he told me that you were going to alleviate his burden to our organisation. Is this correct?'

'I don't know,' The Painter answered.

The Serbian leaned back in his chair. 'Okay fella, I understand you artist types believe you're not privy to the same codes of social conduct as us mere plebeians and so perhaps I can explain the situation for you. Make things a bit clearer, so to speak. My associate here, Miss Olga, acquired training in her homeland at the hands of some ex-KGB men. Do you follow what I'm trying, oh-so-subtly, to convey?'

'KGB?'

Olga's left hand was around The Painter's throat in a pincer-like grip. He hadn't seen her move. His airflow stopped immediately. He started to choke and his head began filling with blood. The pain in his throat was excruciating but he was unable to make any sound other than a slight gargling noise. His head began pounding, his eyes bulged, and his consciousness ebbed. A subtle flick of the Serbian's head and Olga disengaged her hand and leaned back against the desk.

The Painter fell forward against the wood, breathing sporadically and coughing profusely. Costas laughed while Olga checked her fingernails for any signs of damage to her manicure. Tears fell down The Painter's face as he struggled to gain control of his breathing.

'I trust we understand each other now,' The Serbian was saying, as the roaring subsided in The Painter's ears. 'Business doesn't have to be a hardship. There are ways and means of conducting oneself without having to resort to coercive measures.' He sounded disappointed as he opened up the thick, black ledger on his desk and peered inside at one of the pages.

The Painter was still bent over, gripping hold of the edge of the desk. He could feel its smooth, varnished grains. He could smell the sweet hum of Olga's perfume and feel the continued throbbing produced by her grip.

Costas closed the book and looked over at The Painter. 'Your friend owes us a considerable sum of money. Are you here to complete repayments for him?'

'Repayments.' The Painter stumbled over the word.

'Do you have the money?' Olga demanded.

The Painter lifted himself up, put his hand in his pocket and took out all the cash he had on him. He held it out. Costas took the money and flicked through it. He then smiled at Olga.

Before The Painter saw the movement, her hand smacked him hard across the back of his head, sending his neck reeling forward and his chin bouncing painfully off the desk.

'This ain't gonna do it, fella,' Costas announced as he pushed the money back towards The Painter. 'We're going to have to come to a more amicable arrangement. One which is more beneficial to us.'

The Painter's head was swelling. He could hardly focus

any more with his right eye. His chin and head were aching in unison.

Costas opened one of the drawers in his desk and pulled out a bottle of clear spirits. He also retrieved two small shot glasses. 'Let's try a different tack, shall we? Before you have an aneurism.' He placed the shot glasses on the desk and unscrewed the bottle top. He poured out two full measures of the spirit and passed one to The Painter. 'Drink up,' he instructed. 'Don't worry, it's not poison. It's good quality vodka.' He slung his own measure back in one gulp.

The Painter picked up his glass and sipped at it. The burning in his throat merged with the pain emanating from everywhere else. He tipped the remains back and coughed, spluttering out hard.

'It's good stuff, no?' The Serbian laughed as he poured out another two measures. He threw his second back as swiftly and as effortlessly as he had the first. The Painter gripped his glass with all the force he could muster and slammed the liquid down his throat.

'There you go. Doesn't that feel better?' Costas smiled.

The Painter rolled his glass along the table-top in response. The vodka was making its way through his body and into his head. The intensity of the situation blurred a little, as did the physical expanse of the room. The brightness of the light seemed to dim slightly, too. His stomach remained queasy and his nerves striated from the beatings dished out by Olga, who sat quietly awaiting further instruction.

'Let's start again, shall we?' Costas suggested. 'We're going to have to come to some kind of compromise here. One that is, let us say, mutually beneficial to all parties. Now this friend of yours, Dan Smithson, owes us £50,000. He has proposed that you will clear his debt. That debt has now been passed on to you.'

'To me?' The Painter enquired.

Olga lowered her face close to his. 'If you interrupt one more time, I'm going to take the heel of my shoe and shove it so far up your ass it's going to break your teeth.'

The Serbian motioned towards Olga. 'You're going to have to get a grip on things here, fella. Olga is not to be fucked with. She can keep you alive and in exquisite pain for an indeterminate period of time. It is not an edifying sight, believe me.'

The Painter restrained himself into silence.

'I have a proposal for you,' Costas began. 'It doesn't involve money, but the transfer of goods. Here is how we are going to resolve this minor dispute. I hear that you are a world-renowned artist and that your paintings exchange hands for considerable sums. One was sold just yesterday which fetched a rather handsome amount. What I therefore propose is that you,' he pointed directly at The Painter, 'produce a picture for us in exchange for your life.'

The Painter looked at Olga before answering, seeking permission. She looked straight ahead.

He took the risk. 'A picture?'

'Of course. This is the most equitable solution possible. You have chosen to take on Dan Smithson's debt. You don't have the necessary finances to reimburse us and so I propose you relinquish this debt in the form of a painting. You will make this painting for us and deliver it in no less than one week from today. It doesn't matter if the paint isn't quite dry. What matters is the quality of the piece. Which brings me swiftly on to the next matter at hand. We have people who are in the position of verifying as to the provenance of this picture. In other words, if you get one of your studio assistants, or your girlfriend or your grandmother, to knock up a painting for you, we'll know. Then you'll have Olga to answer to. Do you know what Olga's going to do to you?'

'No.'

'She's going to tie you down naked and then she's

going to take a thin razor blade and split your scrotum open with it. Then she's going to pop your testicles out, one at a time, while you watch. Next, she's going to pop those balls onto a metal skewer with some peppers and onions and mushrooms. She's going to smear over some sticky, sweet and spicy barbecue sauce and she's going to spit-roast them over a grill, as you watch. Then she's going to feed them to me. It's an unforgettable experience. Of course, more so for you than for anybody else. And then Olga is really going to hurt you. She's going to serve you up to me over the course of the next twenty-four hours, by which time you'll have finally succumbed to the relative serenity of death. Do we understand one another?'

'You want me to make you a picture?' The Painter asked, confused.

He received a full-on slap to the left side of his face from Olga in reply. His head ricocheted to the right and back again before the ringing in his ear blotted all other senses. Blood from his eye began dripping down his face. More blood began to form on his tongue where he had bitten it. His tastebuds were overpowered by a metallic stodge as he spat some out across the desk.

Olga's long, thin heel met with his genitals and he bowled over into a heaped mass on the floor. She swiftly dragged him off the rug, hitting his head on the doorpost. The Painter lay there, semi-conscious. The room swelled up and began to devour him. He could see the scuffed marks in the wood of the skirting boards, a few food crumbs lying on the floor, and then the blood dribbling out of his mouth.

He started to cough violently and some of the blood-spattered Olga's patent leather shoes. In return she kicked him hard in the chest, then began to rub the blood off on his suit jacket.

She knelt down and placed her face by The Painter's. 'You are a miserable piece of shit. You're going to paint this picture or I'm going to kill you.'

The Painter looked pleadingly towards Costas.

'Don't look at him. He's not going to save you. That prick Smithson borrowed my money and you're going to pay it back. You're going to do me a painting and I better get a good price for it. Because if I don't, I'm going to come looking for you. And what I'm going to do to you is going to be so much worse than that little scenario Costas painted for you. If I don't get an artwork from you I'm going to turn you into one instead. I'm going to skin you alive and turn you into a fucking rug, which I'm going to use to wipe my feet on every time I stand on some dog shit. Do you understand?' Olga moved away from The Painter and turned to Costas. 'Get this smear of scum off the floor and out of this office.'

Costas helped The Painter up off the floor, through the office to the door. Once in the corridor, he left him leaning up against the wall. The Painter looked askance at Costas with his one decent eye. 'Dan Smithson,' he said. 'I don't have his address.'

Costas stared at The Painter and a smirk slid across his lips momentarily. He pulled a small pad and pen from his pocket and scribbled something on it. He took the piece of paper, tore it from the pad, folded it up neatly and placed it in The Painter's top pocket. He patted the pocket kindly after placing it there.

'Try not to get any blood on the walls, or in the lift, eh fella,' he told The Painter before disappearing back into the office and closing the door.

CHAPTER 14

The Painter tried to move but rebounded off the opposite wall. He tried desperately to cling on to the plaster and hold himself upright. Instead, his upper body slumped against it. His knees jack-knifed and he crumpled to the floor. The nasty green carpet tiles itched their way against his palms. He rubbed the scabbing wound on his left hand against their coarse grain, leaving pieces of dead flesh in their wake. He was now bleeding from the hand, the head, and the mouth. He stared down at the clean, glorious red that was coursing from his palm. He pushed it onto his white t-shirt and streaked it across the cotton fibres in a semi-circular motion. He then spat out across the yellow enamelled wall and used his right index finger to join the spots of spittle together in a unified collage.

The Painter started to move crab-like along the wall towards the lift. He suckered his palms against the plaster and shuffled his feet along. He couldn't open his legs very far, due to the kick from Olga. Every piece of his anatomy felt as though it was in a spasm of protracted nerve-endings, pulsing through a series of electrified, explosive charges. He tried moving his neck, legs and arms to loosen the tension, but it simply caused him further pain. The immensity of the task of simply reaching the lift rendered it seemingly impossible.

He froze momentarily and panted into the wall. His stale, garlicky breath rolled across the heavy surface. It rebounded into his nostrils and made his stomach retch. The burning of the chillies and the vodka careened up from his stomach, firing gastric acid into his oesophagus. The Painter groaned at the pain, which acted as a spur to getting him moving, and he lurched towards the lift.

He pressed the button to summon the elevator, hitting harder a second time. The button lit up but he continued to hit it several more times. The whirring of the mechanism kicked into place and the elevator chugged upwards. When it finally came to a rest on his floor, the doors clattered open. Standing inside, waiting, was the same large, sweating man, with the grey, tobacco-ridden comb-over and brown kipper tie. He smiled sweetly for The Painter as he held the doors in place for him to enter. Once inside, The Painter turned to see the sweating man had already disappeared into the labyrinthine corridor.

The Painter hit the button for the ground floor and pinned himself against the back of the lift. The metal beneath his palms was cool and smooth to the touch, except for a few dimples in its skin. His hands began to secrete sweat upon the shiny, metal surface. The blood from his palm left its own imprint on the steel canopy.

The doors initially sprang open partway and then diffidently pushed themselves fully apart. There was nobody waiting to enter this time and The Painter took so long to get through the doors that he had to jam his arms into their sides to stop them from closing.

The gloom of the foyer was more oppressive than it had been before. The tiled flooring was grubby and distressed; the walls a sickly, jaundiced colour, and they held within them the smell of cheap bleach. The entire space had a fevered, malarial quality to it. The Painter staggered towards the exit, desperate to leave the fetid air, drawn by the promise of the bright, cleansing sunlight outside.

The mild afternoon street was lazy and quiet. There were no students or tramps in sight. Two mothers pushed their babies along the pavement, a shopkeeper smoked a cigarette in the street, and the traffic on the road was steady but unhurried.

The Painter wandered over to the car and stopped to read a message left on the passenger side. A single word had been spray-painted in black along its length: 'wanker'. He touched the letter 'n' and ran his finger through it. The paint was dry. He bent forward and smelled it. There was the vaguest trace of a metallic pear-like scent. He took out the car key and held it in his right hand. He started to use it on the 'n', as a means of erasing it. The spray paint and the car's own paint underneath came away. The smoking shopkeeper paused to watch in anxious concern. He seemed to be gesturing something but The Painter paid no attention as he continued to scratch away the letter before he walked around to the driver's side, unlocked the car, and got in.

The inside of the Porsche was warm and the leather interior gave off a mildly masculine odour. The Painter sat behind the wheel and took the piece of paper, given to him by Costas, from his top pocket, and opened it. The small lined sheet held an address, under which was a doodle of a hand, with all the fingers bent over except for the middle one, which was pointed straight up and out at The Painter. He mimicked the drawing with his own hand in silent response.

The Painter started the Porsche and tapped the address of Dan Smithson into the satellite navigation system. He pulled out cautiously into the street but still met the ire of a young motorist in an all-black low-slung hatchback with a large, loud exhaust and blue tinted windows. As he drove down the street, The Painter passed the shopkeeper, who bent down to look inside the car, a puzzled expression etched across his face.

The car negotiated its way through narrow streets, past low-rent housing and dilapidated workshops, until it came onto a wider road down by the river.

The Painter sped his way across a steel-built cantilevered bridge. Coming out from underneath the bridge was a long, glass-topped boat carrying a dozen or so passengers, who were photographing all and sundry. It wasn't the only boat on the river; there were various other vessels navigating the deep, dark expanse of water.

The sun's rays sparkled off the top of the rippling

waves. Their joyful light contrasted directly with the oil-slicked flotsam washing along the very narrow shoreline. The city's detritus heaved up against the embanked walls. The bridge cast a dark shadow, outlining its magnificent architecture across the river. Nature met the mechanised world in a fabled, melancholic silhouette.

The Painter slowed to take hold of the sight. The light bouncing off the water; rubbish piled up at the shore; dark shadows cast by the bridge and the stone banks.

On the other side of the river were mid-storey, solid industrial buildings and glass-fronted offices. There were large, pivoting cranes dancing arabesques in the pale blue skies above the clockwork, perfunctory cityscape below. Construction workers and administration workers scurried around at street-, building site- and office-level. There were buses and taxis ferrying people back and forth from a nearby railway station and two police cars screamed past The Painter's car, sirens wailing through the streets. The pavement's denizens carried on their business without even a flicker of interest in their eyes.

The car navigated its way through a zigzag of streets far removed from the citywide views of the riverfront, to come to a standstill outside an anonymous, grey, plastic-looking block of luxury apartments.

The Painter pulled the Porsche up to the pavement and parked it with two wheels on the kerb in front of Dan Smithson's home address. A man walking along the street stared at the side of the car and smiled. He was followed by two women who read out loud the message written in black paint along the passenger wing of the car.

The Painter stepped out of the vehicle and felt his way around the boot, pinning himself upright until he reached the pavement.

He looked down through the grate of a drain, into the water flowing underneath, down towards the river. The water began to wash and flow back and forth and for a time appeared to stop altogether. It was then that he heard the whispering coming from below and The Painter got down on all fours and bent his ear towards the drain. He could hear the wind passing through the city, underneath its foundations. 'You are part of a whole: everything is connected.'

He put his face closer to the drain. There was a sulphurous quality to the smell that rose to greet him, as though the earth's core had produced a giant belch. He framed his right eye between two bars of the grille. The passing water seemed possessed of a purpose, which it hadn't previously exhibited.

The water had a dull and muddy palette, which would mix well with all the other effluents being pumped into the river, to give it that richly decayed feel, which produced that oily soup so worthy of a mass grave for lonely suicides throughout the centuries.

A middle-aged woman in a jumper, jeans and flat shoes stopped above The Painter. 'Excuse me, are you feeling okay?'

He looked up into her concerned, warm brown eyes. 'Yes.' The Painter scrambled to his feet, holding on to the car to steady himself.

'I'm sorry, I thought you were hurt or ill,' she said, taking in The Painter's bruised and battered face. 'Would you like me to fetch someone or call an ambulance?'

'It's okay. I'm visiting somebody.' The Painter gestured towards the building beside them as means of an explanation.

'Oh. I see,' the woman continued. 'I don't want to disturb you. I just thought that I'd better ask if you needed help.' She smiled, lightly, but the concern never left her eyes as she moved away and carried on down the street.

A young man in a blue pinstriped suit, accessorised with black shoes, a blue shirt and a purple tie, passed The Painter, giving him as wide a berth as possible. His only concern that the dishevelled man might ask him for help.

The Painter made his way to the glass doors of Dan Smithson's building. There was an electronic intercom at the side of the entrance. He pulled the address from his pocket once again and, holding it before him, pressed a button for the corresponding number on the intercom. There was no reply. He tried three times but all to no avail.

He walked to the side of the building where there was a barrier and a slip road leading into an underground garage. The entire building seemed closed off to any unwelcome visitors. The Painter returned to the glass entrance doors and stood waiting attentively for any animated movement going into or out of the building. In his distressed state, he had to prop himself up against a wall to stop himself from collapsing.

The Painter rubbed at his right eye and dabbed at his left. The swelling was still growing and it shot a wave of pain up into his cranium. He held his head in his hands in an attempt to stop it falling towards the ground and lying there, motionless, for eternity. His legs felt as though they could detach themselves and his body could levitate freely without their encumbrance. They rippled and wrinkled fatigue all the way up from his feet through his calves to his thighs. The continuing ache from his testicles went down to meet it. His arm muscles could hardly feel to grip and his torso felt painfully aware of the mass it was underpinning and carrying. It felt as though it too would dispense with all limbs at will, just to be an iconoclastic piece of corpse freely rolling around in the gutter.

CHAPTER 15

A young woman wearing Lycra and holding a sports bag swiftly exited the building. The Painter was too slow to move and the glass door clicked back and locked just as he grabbed at it. He pushed and pulled the long metal handle for a moment, but it refused to give.

The reflective image cast back at The Painter from the smoky glass stunned him. There was no longer anything left of his former self to recognise. The face before him was so worn and weathered that he looked like a boxer stumbling from the ring, defeated and brain-damaged. His pallor was all blacks, blues, reds and purples. The skin was bumped, pinched, scratched and scarred.

The Painter held his right palm out to the reflection and the glass bent tepidly inwards. His right eye was fluttering and the left still blind. Waves of tension rolled over his stomach in quick succession. The faces of those who passed by on the street seemed normal and serene in comparison. He looked as though someone had pulled his face back to reveal a cancerous, ripped lesion. Sitting above his head in the reflection was a lamp-post and directly behind him, further down the street, a small roundabout.

He turned away from the glass door and resumed his position of watchfulness by the side of the entrance. Cars passed along the road and pedestrians passed along the street, but there was no movement from inside or outside the building. The Painter began to crouch down on his haunches to try and relieve some of the tension and fatigue that were plaguing him.

Suddenly the door opened and a man dressed casually in jeans and a chequered shirt appeared. He kept the door open, using his back, as he texted on his mobile phone. The Painter took his opportunity and stumbled into action, banging into the man as he attempted to enter the building.

The man wouldn't let him past and looked up from his phone. 'Can I help you, pal? Who are here to see?'

'Dan Smithson,' The Painter announced hopefully.

The man searched The Painter's face and his own memory. 'Oh yeah, the art critic guy.' He pointed at The Painter and wagged his finger. 'I know you. I've seen you being interviewed on television. You're an artist, aren't you?'

'Artist?' The Painter asked.

The man moved out of the way for him and held the door open. 'Okay, on you go, then. I hope you're not here to do him any harm, because of a bad review he's written about you.'

The Painter looked back at the man, who chuckled at his own joke then patted him on the shoulder. 'Don't worry. I'm not bothered, he seems like a bit of a tosser, to be honest.'

The Painter moved inside the building without comment, as the man walked off jovially, still texting on his phone.

Standing in the foyer of the building, The Painter made his way to the brightly-lit, enclosed stairway. He clumped his way exhaustedly upwards, reaching the top of the first two flights. A metal plaque outside a fire door stated apartments 1–4. He slogged his way up the next two flights to reach numbers 5–8, then another two flights to 9–12, and then the final two flights to apartments 13–16.

By the completion of his journey, The Painter was exhausted and could not endure another step. He sat down on the top stair by the glass-and-wood fire door. As he sat panting, he heard the click of the entrance door, then the quick rush of footsteps. Another door opened and closed on the second floor and the building became quiet again, but for his heavy, laboured breathing.

He felt underneath the fitted piece of plastic grip protecting the edges of each stair. He ripped at it with his fingers, but it would not budge. The walls were painted an off-white colour and on the ceiling were large, light-radiating ceiling lamps. The whole place was clean and sterile. It had no overall smell or texture and felt very cold and perfunctory.

The Painter finally managed to haul himself upwards and push open the door separating the stairway from the living quarters. The corridor inside was as brightly-lit and uneventful as the stairwell. There were two doors on either side. The first on the left had the number 13 on it and a small doorbell to the side. The Painter pressed it once and waited. There was no answer forthcoming. He pressed it again, twice in quick succession. There was still no answer. He tried the handle and the door pushed inwards.

The Painter followed it inside. To his left was a metal stand holding two umbrellas, one black and one red. Against the wall a low, long, white wooden bookshelf was overflowing with thick magazines and journals. Towards the back of the room a raised area had two steps leading up to it. It held a black leather armchair next to a small, square glass coffee table. On the back wall was a glass sliding door with white Venetian blinds. Outside, a small grey metal patio area was dressed with an orange metal bistro table and two matching chairs. Also in view was a small compact kitchen with black cupboards and black marbled work surfaces, which held a filter coffee machine, a kettle and a toaster, all in burnished metal. The sink was made of stainless steel and had an empty, metal dish-dryer next to it and a wooden knife-holder filled with black-handled kitchen blades. On the wall above the bookshelf was a framed black-and-white photographic portrait of an old man with sunken, piercing eyes in a thin, gaunt face, deeply creased skin, and thick grey hair which stuck up like a brush. He resembled a handsome, human vulture.

To the right of the door, the living area was taken up by a brown suede two-seater sofa, with a rectangular wooden coffee table sitting square in the centre of a brown, shag-pile wool rug. A giant lamp arched over the sofa, which was pointed towards a large, grey plasma television fixed to the wall. Further bookshelves filling two perpendicular walls towards the back of the room, filled with novels and art books, providing a backdrop to a round tulip-shaped white table and four white plastic chairs with metal, tower-like legs.

The Painter entered the space fully and noticed an unexpected addition to the room. There was a naked, dead body nailed to the floorboards. Lying fully splayed out, palms and feet pinned down to the wooden floorboards, his neck garrotted and sliced open at the front by use of the piano wire still attached noose-like around his throat, his penis in a fully erect position and with what looked like a magazine wedged into his anus, was the late art critic Dan Smithson.

The Painter couldn't move. His arms and legs trembled and his face began to sweat. As he took in the sight, the deteriorating remains of his lunch splattered out over the floor in front of him. The Painter looked down at the partially-digested food particles. They were the last thing he saw before everything went black.

CHAPTER 16

The heavy throbbing turned into an insatiable pounding as The Painter cracked open a listless right eye. His brain was punching his left eye with a vengeful ferocity, but still it would not open. It felt as if the organ was trying desperately to escape the prison of his skull, which held it in tormented, painful captivity. To be free of the ceaseless misery of those waves of steel blades slicing through his head. In between the pain, The Painter could vaguely make out a feeling of dampness and the bile-ridden stench of the vomit in his nostrils.

He managed to turn far enough to stare at the top of the head of Dan Smithson. He could see naked shoulders, arms spread out, and the hands which had been partially nailed to the floor. The nail heads were sticking out about an inch from his flesh. They were round and made of metal, which glimmered a little in the early evening light. They had been hammered in mercilessly and had bent due to the exertion. There were small pools of blood on the floor, next to Dan Smithson's hands, due to the deep wound that he had sustained in his neck. His legs were splayed widely and the feet similarly attached to the wooden floor.

The Painter tried to reach out, to touch Dan Smithson's hair, his flesh, his body. His right arm crept painfully forwards into a disjointed posture and he tried rattling it a little. While his muscles ached, the limb didn't seem to be broken. His neck didn't have the strength to prise itself from the floor. The Painter lay still in the vomit and the blood stemming from the gash on his left eyebrow, which had re-opened when he fell.

The Painter crunched up the toes on both feet to check he wasn't paralysed and flexed the fingers on his left hand to convince himself that nothing was broken there either. As well as the searing pain in his head there were convulsions of pain attacking the left side of his jaw.

His mouth had that now familiar mixture of blood and vomit swilling around in it. He attempted to spit, but could only manage to gargle some bloodied, puke-laden froth from the left side of his mouth, which immediately started to run back through his lips, causing him to choke and cough. He rolled onto his back, but this seemed to exacerbate the pain in his head and the choking in his throat. With a gargantuan effort, The Painter flipped himself back over and onto all fours.

In this position, he had the vantage of witnessing Dan Smithson's corpse more fully. He looked at the greying, mottled skin; the bulging eyes; the protruding, swollen tongue, and the incongruously erect penis. The nails that held Dan Smithson's feet to the floor were bent. The length of piano wire lay haphazardly on the floor, a hooked coil at one end.

The Painter clung to the sofa as he slowly got to his feet. The smooth, warm material was comforting; a contrast to the macabre scene set out before him. He put his left hand into his mouth and felt a loose molar. He wobbled the tooth back and forth until it sucked up out of its cavity and came free in his hand. His mouth immediately began filling up with the sickly iron taste of fresh blood. He held the detached tooth in front of his face. It was white and cracked, with roots dangling beneath, festering in gore. The Painter looked closer and noticed a small piece of food stuck in its crown. He flicked it free with his nail and cleaned the roots on his sleeve. Then he placed the tooth back into his mouth and rolled it around, before swallowing it whole.

Taking his first tentative steps, The Painter crept towards the cadaver. He stopped beside the torso and glanced down at the frozen, terror-filled eyes of Dan Smithson. The glasses were gone but it was him alright. The same head, the same face, and the same eyes, only dead. His tongue had ballooned out and took up the entire entrance to his mouth. The Painter could now witness for himself the sheer devastation that the piano wire's noose had visited on Smithson's neck. It had been pulled so ferociously tight that it had ripped right into the throat and flesh surrounding it. There was a purpling ring of sinew hanging onto the wire.

The Painter knelt down and took stock of the carnage inflicted upon Dan Smithson: the garrotting, the nails through hands and feet. He curiously observed the erect penis. He tapped it with the knuckle of his right index finger. It moved slightly, but he didn't repeat the action. Instead, he leaned over and pulled the rolled-up magazine from Smithson's anus. Some fluid escaped immediately afterwards and trickled down from the space left. When The Painter unfurled the magazine he could see the end was soaked in a brown substance that indicated Dan Smithson had soiled himself at some point. The magazine was *Art and Culture*. There was the picture of the African mask that The Painter recognised from his own copy.

He felt the urge to touch the corpse. He stroked along the cold, taut skin of a body devoid of any warmth or human feeling. He pinched at the flesh and it began to give way and crumple a little. The smell was already becoming more pungent. He looked at the horror-stricken face and that cold, greying, swollen tongue. He bent over and put his mouth over it. It had a stale, putrid feel. The Painter spat it out and vomited again, coating Dan Smithson's face, before trying to clean up the mess with his sleeve.

The Painter gathered himself up onto his feet with a debilitating surge of energy. Once standing, he placed the magazine on the dusty white table. The faecal matter staining the magazine dribbled onto the furniture's plastic surface. He felt along the table's manmade coating; it was as cold and desolate as the corpse on the floor. He fell down into one of the chairs and lay with his head stacked into his folded arms on the table top.

He lifted his eyes far enough to witness the bloodstains that led through the living space into the small corridor beyond. The Painter rose to his feet and started to follow the deep red trail. The blood and shit had left a muddy, autumnal passage through that room and into the bedroom beyond.

A double bed clothed in grey sheets was stained copiously with Dan Smithson's bodily matter. The duvet was lying on the floor beside the bed. There were doors to the left forming a fitted wardrobe and to the right was a small black desk holding a silver laptop computer, and a black leather chair placed on castors. Beside the bed there was another small bookcase filled with travel guides. The window had the same wooden Venetian blinds as the balcony window. They cut the room into varying shafts of light, which fell along the wall and the bed, on which there was a solid wooden headboard, also slatted with beams of wood.

The Painter sat on the edge of the bed amongst the carnage of the slaying. He dipped his finger in a small pool of blood and wiped it along a clean piece of cotton. Then he took another sample of Smithson's blood and joined it with his own in the wound to his eye which Emily had given him. He briefly pondered how he might paint the scene, using blood mingled with paint for The Serbian's commission and the symmetry of including the bodily fluids of a man The Serbian had clearly murdered.

The smell in the room was dark and earthy. There was the blood and the excrement, but there was also a wider scent of decomposition: life made dead.

The Painter looked around the room, noting the bedside lamp which lay smashed on the floor. In the wall above the bed was a line that marked out a large square. The paint inside the line seemed newer and fresher than that on the outside. There were also mounting holes on the wall. The Painter stood up and walked towards the paint square.

Something was missing; something which had taken pride of place above the bed. He moved his hand along the wall, in between the demarcation line. The wall felt exactly the same on both sides of the line. The paintwork was smooth and cool to the touch. It moved from a bright white to a slightly murkier one. He looked down and noticed a well-thumbed travel guide to Mexico on the small wooden bedside table. On the floor was the silver foil wrapper of an unused condom.

The Painter wandered out of the bedroom and back into the living space. Dan Smithson's body remained resolutely nailed to the floor. His positioning was exactly the same as when The Painter had first entered the flat. The only difference was that his face was slicked with vomit. The Painter watched his lips as they appeared animated for a moment, 'It is you who are responsible for yourself'.

He could see the skeleton straining to penetrate outwards: to shed itself of the now dead and burdensome flesh. The Painter took his right index finger and softly sketched around the outline of the body pinned to the floor. He could feel it melting away before his eyes, seeping down into the cracks in the flooring, draining itself into the flat below and then onwards into the soil beneath the building. The body's ephemera mingling seamlessly with his own lifeblood, unseen, to feed the city below.

The Painter finally turned his face away from the corpse and started to walk to the door. On his way out, he slipped briefly on the wooden floor from the gore attached to the soles of his feet. He exited swiftly.

Outside in the corridor, the air felt significantly lighter and more pleasant. He could breathe properly for the first time since he had entered Dan Smithson's apartment. The Painter held himself against the wall, pushing his lungs in and out in an exaggerated gesture. The pain still throbbed around his head and his body was as fatigued as it had been for days. The mugginess of the vodka had been replaced by the blurriness caused by his experience inside the art critic's flat. In a myopic haze, he began to descend the stairs by clinging on to the walls. He clumped his way downwards, one tentative step at a time, one flight after another. His hand dashed the clinical walls, leaving a speckling of blood here and there.

It was rapidly darkening outside and a light drizzle had settled in. People out in the street were scurrying back and forth, heads down, gunning for home.

He opened the door and found himself in the full maelstrom of rush hour. The traffic in the road was more congested and polluted than before. People were leaving and entering buildings all around the encircling streets in a whirlwind of choreographed randomness.

A young woman in a beige Mackintosh coat and large brown handbag clamped under her arm swished past The Painter and into the building he had just come from. His presence drew little attention from the urban mutineers now surrounding him.

The car lights were on and the horns were in full use. People bobbed their way through the weaving traffic as the quickest route to the other side of the street. The more cautious used the traffic lights further along the road.

The surrounding offices and flats blazed with light, illuminating the street. People worked, walked home, caught taxis, bought goods, cooked dinner, and fluttered into a scattering of bars, cafés and restaurants, as he stood there unseen. Nobody paused, nobody stopped; it was an ordered sense of chaos.

The picture was of an overall miasma of muted blues and browns, whites and greys, beiges and blacks. The red of the car lights and the colours of the traffic lights were an aberration in a storm of blankness. The street was making The Painter's one working eye lazy and he felt dizzy.

He pinned himself back against the wall of the

apartment building and counted the cracks on the pavement that separated him from the Porsche. It became an abstract ordering of geometric patterns constantly washed over by the feet of the passing pedestrians. He looked up and glimpsed their faces as they flooded past him in an uncertain haze.

He started to feel the evening chill and shuddered to himself. The people on the street avoided his gaze and the bruised and battered, cut and corrupted figure he projected.

He observed the shadows of people caught quickly in the light which glazed the concrete fleetingly. It seemed as though those dark splashes were swept down under the pavement and transferred into the bowels of the world.

The Painter fished around in his pocket for the car key. He mustered all his resources and pushed himself forward onto the street. He was narrowly missed by a car, whose driver instantly communicated his disapproval with several bursts of his horn. He managed to scramble his way into the Porsche and sat holding his pounding head for a few moments while the pain subsided enough for him to be able to drive. He placed his own address in the satellite navigation and pulled the Porsche into the traffic, eliciting several reprimands from other drivers.

He followed the car's instructions to turn the car around in the middle of the road, causing him to narrowly miss a man with a black umbrella, who angrily kicked the passenger door. Other drivers remonstrated with him by any means possible as he accelerated out of trouble, driving straight through a red light.

His entire journey home was hampered by the endless yawn of rush-hour traffic. He moved torturously slowly over a stone bridge on the river. From inside the car's luxurious cockpit, he watched the mass of muddy water darken slowly in the last vestiges of the fading light. The city began to take over the waterway, throwing its myriad lights sparkling across it. Boats still ferried their way up and down, keeping their own lights ablaze.

He moved past the grand edifices of the more ancient stone buildings in the old quarter of the city. The buildings here were a bulwark against the entropic carnage of the streets below. There was a symmetry, an order and a confidence in those streets, in contrast to other areas of the urban sprawl. The denizens of these spaces pushed through the pavements and carried themselves with a seemingly haughty disdain for their fellow citizens.

By the end of his journey the sky was awash with an orange glow and he was fighting sleep. The Painter stopped the Porsche outside his building and turned off the engine. He swiftly untangled himself from the vehicle and eloped onto the pavement.

The nightshift across the road was buzzing into full production. Vans were coming and going with carcasses heaving their way into the large, cavernous building, to be dispatched by razor-sharp cleavers and knives into every joint and cut of meat possible.

The red, gorged flesh seemed effervescent to The Painter's eye in comparison with Dan Smithson's dull-eyed, greying corpse. The smell from the animals across the street had been cleansed of decay; they were now fresh and vibrant gourmand fodder in the hands of the butchers. It was death remade as joyful entertainment.

In the city's streets the night was drying out. The slick of rain which coated the pavements was slowly disintegrating in the deep glow of the streetlamps. The Painter moved towards his building but was obstructed by the sight of two men. Both wore grey suits, one dark and one light. The one in the dark suit wore a light grey tie and light grey shoes. The one sporting the light grey suit was dressed in a dark grey tie and dark grey shoes. The one in the dark suit had light brown skin, the other was a pale white. They both appeared to be around the same age, in their mid-thirties.

The man in the dark grey suit advanced first. He held out a card. 'I'm Detective McMann.' He gestured to the other man in the light grey suit. who also advanced, 'And this is Detective McMinn.' He looked at the Porsche. 'Is this your car?'

'It's Hans'.' The Painter replied.

Detective McMinn walked over to the car. 'Hans Zimmer?'

'Yes.'

The detective pulled a black-and-yellow striped packet from the window. He held it aloft. 'Someone's been a naughty boy.'

Detective McMann stood facing The Painter. 'We need to talk to you about Hans Zimmer.'

'Okay.' The Painter tried to move towards the building.

Detective McMinn laughed and shook his head as he moved towards the other two men. 'Cute. Very cute.'

The other detective stopped The Painter. 'Not in there, sir. Down at the station if you please.'

The two detectives started to walk towards a standard black saloon car. Detective McMann strode in front of The Painter and Detective McMinn took up the rear.

The Painter stumbled his weary way towards the car and as he approached it, the back door was politely held open by Detective McMann. 'Sit in there please, sir.'

The Painter bent into the car and knocked his head on the way in, before slumping on the back seat.

'Mind your head, sir,' Detective McMann cautioned. He shut the door and looked at the other detective. Both men shook their heads.

'Long night, huh?' McMinn said.

'Oh, yeah,' McMann returned on his behalf.

The two police officers got into the front of the unmarked vehicle, McMann driving and McMinn in the passenger seat.

CHAPTER 17

The Painter leaned his head back against the car seat and closed his one good eye. The car had a stale, neutral smell. The seat covering was clean but uninspiring. The hum of the engine was dull and quiet. The detectives said nothing to him, they just faced forwards towards their destination. The Painter's breathing slowed and the pull of sleep was too much for him to resist. The car began gliding along the tarmac, pushing and pulling his stomach inwards. The ring of darkness drew greater towards the coal-black centre. It drew him further and further in, whizzing past the charcoal greys at the outer rim and on into that deep hollow abyss which was rapidly encircling his entire periphery.

Although his eye was still closed, he could hear the conversation of the two men in front. He refused to contemplate the world outside of his dark inner expanse, due to the pain piercing finely calibrated holes his skull.

'So it's not going to go anywhere?'

'No, I don't think so.'

'Why not?'

'Honestly? I think she's too prejudiced.'

'Against you being black?'

'No, oh no, not that. She's not like that. I think she's prejudiced against me being a police officer.'

'I've had that before a few times.'

'Well, she's a liberal lawyer. You know the type. They think we're all fascists.'

'You need to get the right one. You know, bust out the old uniform and the handcuffs.'

'Amen to that.'

Both men laughed.

The Painter eventually managed to induce his right eye to open and hauled himself up a little in his seat. None of these movements reduced the pain factor in his body: his head hurt, his face hurt, his neck hurt, his hand hurt, his fingers hurt, his stomach hurt. He even felt one of his testicles and it appeared to be swollen.

Detective McMinn turned around to survey him.

'Morning, sleepyhead,' he said.

They pulled in through black, painted metal gates and the car came to a stop outside a brightly-lit, nondescript building.

'Here we are,' Detective McMann announced.

'Home, sweet home.' Detective McMinn smiled at The Painter.

Both the officers exited the vehicle in the same instant, as though choreographed. A few seconds later the back door was opened by Detective McMann.

'This way, sir,' he offered politely.

The Painter stepped out of the vehicle. This time Detective McMann physically ensured that he didn't bash his head by using his warm palm as a barrier while The Painter disembarked.

Out in the forecourt of the building, Detective McMinn stretched himself before turning to The Painter. 'Okay, Picasso, let's go.'

The two policemen led him to a doorway on the left side of the building. The uniformed officer stationed at a reception desk inside buzzed them inside.

The reception area was enclosed. On two walls, notice-boards displayed various posters asking for information regarding specific crimes along with some generic advice and a few anonymous numbers. The office beyond was cut off by a glass partition beginning above the wooden reception desk. To the side of the full partitioning wall there was a door.

The same officer who had buzzed them into the building also buzzed them through the second door. It was bright inside; banks of fluorescent lights cut into the ceiling left few lurking shadows.

There was a small office area immediately through the

doorway, its three desks empty. There was also a bank of small television screens playing endless footage gathered from CCTV cameras strategically spaced around the building.

The Painter looked at the image from outside in the forecourt where they had just been and noticed the large raindrops now showering down, gracefully highlighted against the dour, floodlit space.

A senior female officer, in full uniform, brown hair pinned back in a simple knot at the base of her neck, walked into the office from the corridor beyond, carrying some papers in her left hand. She stopped in front of the detectives and The Painter. She quickly surveyed him and enquired about their prisoner's general demeanour.

'What happened to him?' Her voice held an unnerving suspicion.

'We found him like this,' answered McMinn.

'He looks like he could do with a trip to the hospital.' She scowled, apparently not entirely convinced by the detective's response.

Detective McMann moved aside and indicated to the senior officer that he would like to discuss the matter more privately. She duly obliged, one eye on their prisoner.

The Painter watched as they took a few moments to discuss the options and their various opinions. In the meantime, Detective McMinn ran through some papers lying open on one of the desks. The senior officer appeared to have acquiesced to Detective McMann's assurances with regard to The Painter's wellbeing and moved off to confer with the duty officer on a separate matter.

McMann returned to the fold. 'Okay then, let's go and clear this little matter up.'

The Painter followed Detective McMann into the long corridor with Detective McMinn in hot pursuit. The three men halted outside the third office along and Detective McMann opened the door.

The room was small and bright. Made up of four white walls unbroken by windows, it held a rectangular grey table, two grey plastic chairs on either side. Situated at the far side of the table, towards the wall, was a digital recording device. On the right upper corner of the room, a CCTV camera silently surveyed this space.

The Painter was invited to sit at the side of the table farthest from the door. Detectives McMinn and McMann sat opposite him and McMinn set the digital device on to record.

Indicating the date, the time, and the names of those present, McMann began by asking The Painter: 'Do you know why you're here?'

'No.'

'You don't know why we picked you up?'

'No.'

'Do you know a man by the name of Hans Zimmer?'

'I think so.'

McMinn interjected. 'You think so, or you know so?'

'I think I do.'

'When we picked you up we asked you whose Porsche you were driving and you said Hans Zimmer's.' McMann stated.

'Yes.'

'Yes what?' McMinn asked.

'Yes, it's Hans' car.'

'So, you do know Hans Zimmer?'

'I don't know.'

McMann took over. 'You know it's Hans Zimmer's Porsche, but you don't know if you know Hans Zimmer. Is that correct?'

'Yes.'

'So, the obvious question is: how do you know it's Hans Zimmer's car?'

'I was told it was.'

'By whom?'

'Urs.'

The two detectives looked at each other. McMann asked: 'Urs who?'

'Von something.'

'This guy Urs,' McMann started.

'Urs. Is that a man or a woman?' McMinn butted in.

'A man.'

Detective McMann continued. 'So, this guy Urs von something, told you that the Porsche belongs to Hans Zimmer?'

'Yes.'

'And how does he know?'

'Know what?'

'That the Porsche belongs to Hans Zimmer.'

'I don't know. He wanted to speak to Hans.'

'What about?'

'China.'

McMinn looked perplexed. 'Urs von something wants to speak to Hans Zimmer about China?'

'Yes. Either that or about a piece of furniture.'

'A piece of furniture?' asked Detective McMinn.

'Like a Chinese cabinet or some type of thing like that?' McMann asked.

'I don't know.'

'This whole conversation is starting to feel like a game of Chinese whispers,' McMinn interjected impatiently.

'You know you have Hans Zimmer's Porsche because Urs von something told you so. Is that correct?' Detective McMann asked.

'Yes.'

'But you don't know if you know Hans Zimmer or not?'

'No.'

'How did you come by the car?'

'I don't understand.'

McMinn stepped in. 'Where did you find the car?'

'In a garage.'

'Hans Zimmer's garage?' McMann asked.

'I don't know.' The Painter squinted, the bright light above him seemed to be flashing in time with the pounding in his head.

'You don't know an awful lot,' Detective McMinn announced, frustrated.

'You still don't know why you're here?' Detective McMann asked.

'No.' The Painter watched the light throb and wondered if he would vomit.

'We're conducting a murder investigation here,' McMann told him. 'And you are our chief suspect at the moment. So, if I were you, I would start cooperating with us. This will get you nowhere in the long term. We need some answers from you and you're going to start giving us some. And I don't mean this vague yes and no shit, either. I mean proper, explanatory answers. Do you understand?'

'I don't know.' The Painter said.

'You listen to us, you little prick. My partner is telling you that you're wanted for murder,' McMinn interjected.

'Murdering who?'

'Who do you think?' McMann said as he watched The Painter. His one open eye seemed a little unfocused. Perhaps he did need to see a doctor.

'I don't know.'

McMann and McMinn glanced at each other before McMann continued. 'Hans Zimmer is dead.'

'And we think you killed him,' McMinn added.

'Did you?' Pursued McMann

'No.' The Painter fought an urge to shrug in answer.

'Now we're getting somewhere,' Detective McMann stated.

McMinn began summing up for the benefit of their prisoner. 'You don't admit to knowing Hans Zimmer. But you do admit to taking his car. You know this car, the Porsche, belonged to Hans Zimmer because Urs von something told you it did. This Urs von something wants to speak to Hans Zimmer about China, or furniture, or Chinese furniture. Can we therefore take it as read that this Urs von something does know Hans Zimmer?'

'I don't know.'

McMann continued, 'But he knows the Porsche belongs to Hans Zimmer and he wants to speak to him for various reasons, which at this point we can't properly establish, ergo he must know Hans Zimmer.'

The Painter looked back at them blankly.

'It seems fairly logical he must know him. He knows his car,' McMann responded for him.

'He wants to discuss geography or home furnishings with him,' prompted McMinn.

'How else would he know these things unless he knew Hans Zimmer?' McMann continued.

'I don't know?'

'You're giving us the real runaround here, pal,' Detective McMinn was ready to bounce The Painter's head off the wall.

'Runaround?'

'Yes. The fucking runaround.'

Detective McMann held out a hand to calm his fellow officer before turning to The Painter. 'You want me to tell you a story? Well, okay then, here it is. We see lots of guys like you in here.'

'Loads of them.' McMinn corroborated.

'And it's always the same thing. They think we're idiots. They think they're super clever and we're a bunch of dunces.' McMinn nodded his agreement with his colleague. 'There's a guy commits the perfect crime. The perfect murder. He's never going to get caught. Not in a million years are we going to suspect him of this crime, never mind get him sent down for it. This guy, he's got all the angles covered.'

'All the angles,' confirmed McMinn.

'One day his wife ends up dead.'

'Murdered,' Detective McMinn elucidated.

McMann kept going, 'But nobody's going to suspect this guy, the husband. He's got a cast-iron alibi provided by his secretary. So, it couldn't possibly have been him who murdered his wife.'

McMinn shook his head. 'Not a chance.'

'We start to investigate the case. It turns out this man, the husband, took out a second life-insurance policy on his wife just six months before her death, worth a large sum of money.'

'Motive One,' McMinn suggested.

'His alibi is provided by his secretary. A woman he has had a sexual relationship with for the past two years. We know all this because several witnesses confirm it for us. Now we have motive.'

'Motive two.'

'We work the crime scene, speak to a few more witnesses, and we have all the evidence we need. He goes to court, then he goes to prison. The guy that knew he could outsmart us, because he's a criminal mastermind and we're just some dumbass flatfoots, gets his comeuppance. Two years he's sleeping with his secretary and he honestly believes nobody has noticed. He thinks everyone is blind and stupid. Never mind all the bits and pieces of evidence we found at the crime scene connecting him incontrovertibly to the murder.'

'The guy was a fucking idiot,' McMinn added.

'Plain and simple. He thought he was smarter than us and he wasn't.'

'And neither are you,' McMinn told The Painter. 'So why don't you tell us what really happened?'

'I don't know.'

McMinn swallowed down some anger. 'Do you know

what I think happened?' He ignored The Painter's shrug. 'Here's what happened. You turned up at this Hans Zimmer guy's house and you brought with you a new painting to flog him. But he knows your work. He's a connoisseur of art. He looks at it, he examines it, and he knows it's a fake. He knows you've just knocked up a copy for him. So, he refuses to buy it. You start to lose your temper and say how can it be a fake? And he tells you he knows you just knocked out a copy of one of your paintings. At this point you lose your temper. You take this fake painting of yours and you smash it over his head. Then you take a snapped-off piece of the frame and stick it through his neck. He goes down, starts rolling around, blood shoots up everywhere, you panic, run from the scene, and to add insult to injury, steal the guy's Porsche.'

'Does that sound familiar? Is that how it happened?' Detective McMann asked.

'Of course that's what happened,' McMinn announced, case closed.

'No.'

'You're lying.' McMinn retorted.

Detective McMann relaxed back in his chair, 'We'd like to believe you.'

'We want to believe you,' McMinn added.

'But it just doesn't add up,' continued McMann. 'Here we are. There's a dead body. This is no suicide. We know he was murdered. And we have witnesses that can put you at the scene of the crime. We ask you what happened. And you completely clam up on us. This doesn't look good.'

'You look guilty,' McMinn cautioned. 'It looks like you did it. And we think you did, so it's just a matter of us piecing the evidence together to prove that you did.'

Detective McMann was nodding his head. 'You look guilty. We've got a team working the scene at the moment. Whose fingerprints do you think they're going to come up with? Whose hairs? Whose blood?'

McMinn changed tack. 'How did you get that eye? Did Zimmer give it to you?'

'No. Emily did it.'

McMinn and McMann looked at each other.

'Who is Emily?' McMann asked.

'She's a gallerist.'

'She's a gallerist?' McMann repeated.

'And why did she do that to your eye?'

'I don't know.'

'What did she do it with?

'I don't know.'

'When did she do it?'

'Last night.'

'Where?'

'In bed.'

McMann stepped in, 'Whose house? Yours or hers?'

'Mine.'

There was silence for a moment then Detective McMinn spoke. 'She did that to your eye in bed last night and you don't know why she did it or what with, but you know it was her that did it?'

'I think so.'

'Why do you think so? Weren't you there at the time?'

'Yes.'

'So, how can you not know what she did it with?'

'I had a pillow over my face when she did it.'

McMann looked confused. 'You had a pillow over your face?'

'Yes.'

'Well. I've heard it all now,' McMinn said.

'What were you doing at the time?' inquired McMann.

'Having sex.'

Detective McMinn took over. 'You were having sex with this girl Emily and she put a pillow over your face and hit you with something until your eye burst. But you don't know why she did it.'

'No.'

'I've got a few theories.'

'Me too,' said McMann.

'I think she didn't want to have sex with you. I think she asked you to stop having sex with her and I think you ignored her and carried on doing it. So in desperation she tried to push you away with a pillow and when that didn't work she got desperate and tried fending you off by hitting you repeatedly in the eye.'

'Sound familiar?' Detective McMann asked.

'No,' The Painter calmly answered.

'What did she do after you had sex?' McMinn asked.

'She sat on the floor and cried.'

'This is looking worse for you by the minute here,' McMann began. 'First this guy Hans Zimmer turns up dead and you're the chief suspect in the murder. Next you tell us you sustained an injured eye from this girl Emily, while having sex with her, after which she sat on the floor and cried.'

McMinn took up the reins. 'You're some romantic; this isn't painting you in a good light. No pun intended. We get all sorts in here. Every kind of pervert and weirdo that you can imagine. Some guys like that shit. Having women or men beat them up. Some men even pay women or men to beat them up. This isn't something new. Probably been going on since time began. Cavemen getting clubbed by the women in some dark crevice for fun. Who knows? It takes all sorts. But this little scenario you're explaining doesn't sound like one of those incidents.'

'We're not here to morally judge anyone. What someone does in the privacy of their home is their business. It's not our concern,' McMann stated.

'What is our concern, though, is if there has been a crime committed. Which looks very likely in this instance,' McMinn added.

'A crime?' The Painter repeated.

'Yes. A crime. Having sex with someone without their consent is a crime, it's called rape, you know,' said Detective McMinn.

'A very, very serious crime,' cautioned McMann.

'We're going to have to get in touch with this woman Emily and get her side of this story. You say she's a gallerist. What gallery is she a gallerist for?' McMinn asked.

'Francesca's.'

'That's it. That's your information? Francesca's?' McMinn was shaking his head and eyeing The Painter with contempt.

The Painter squirmed in his chair and grimaced with pain. The throbbing was getting louder.

The two officers watched him curiously.

Detective McMann asked. 'What's the matter with you?'

McMinn added, 'The seat not comfortable enough?'

'I injured my balls,' The Painter explained.

'No shit,' said McMinn. 'Did Emily do that?'

'No. It was Olga,' he answered.

'Who's Olga?' McMann asked.

'She works for The Siberian,' The Painter answered.

'The Siberian,' McMann said. 'Is she a prostitute?'

'I don't know. She says she runs the operation,' The Painter looked at the perplexed faces of his interrogators.

'So this guy The Siberian isn't her pimp?' Detective McMinn quizzed him.

'He's Serbian,' The Painter tried to explain.

'You just said he was Siberian,' said Detective McMann. 'Now you're telling us he's really Serbian?'

'Make up your mind. Which one is it?' asked McMinn.

'He said he's Serbian,' The Painter struggled to hear the questions over the banging in his skull. He really was going to vomit.

'What did Olga do to your balls?' McMann interjected.

'Kicked them.'

'Why did she do that?'

'I don't know,' The Painter fiddled with his genitals. They felt bigger than they should.

'I've got a theory,' McMinn said. 'Let's try this out. Your man the Siberian or the Serbian or whatever he is, offered this woman Olga up to you for sex. You get a bit rough, or she doesn't want to do it, but The Siberian or Serbian is making her. Maybe you like it rough. Maybe you get to the end and you don't want to pay. We know what you guys with money are like, you don't want to part with any of it. Whatever happened, she kicks you in the balls. Either way, coupled with your previous revelation about this woman Emily, this is adding to an image we're beginning to receive of you as a sex predator. Who may or may not be raping and abusing these women.'

'It's not such a difficult leap of the imagination considering what you did to Hans Zimmer,' added McMann. 'That was a very angry and very violent person that committed that crime. If they can do that they're probably capable of anything.'

'Prison's a long stretch for a guy like you who's had his ass wiped for him all his life. Murderer, sex offender, the whole lot. That's a tough stretch,' McMinn chipped in.

'He couldn't do it,' McMann said to McMinn.

'No chance,' laughed McMinn.

'I didn't do anything.'

'That's not how this all looks. We'll have to investigate these incidents with the women. As for the murder. We've got a man looking at the painting that killed Hans Zimmer right now. He's an art expert and he'll be able to tell if its fake. If it's some copy you've knocked out to con him, then it doesn't look good for you,' Detective McMann advised The Painter.

The Painter felt along the desk with the palm of his

hand. It had been scraped, scratched and scarred all along its surface. The plastic chair was uncomfortable and the bright light was badly blinding his already weary eye.

The two men sat in their grey suits, looking perfectly in tune with their surroundings: cold, bland and unconnected. They were both clean-shaven and carried with them a whiff of aftershave and mildly minty breath.

McMann reached over to the digital recording machine and announced that the interview had been suspended. He leaned over to McMinn and conversed with him briefly in a very slight voice, unintelligible to The Painter.

McMinn stood and left the interview room without comment. Then McMann stood up and looked at The Painter. 'Okay, we're going to have to check out a few things here. You're not being charged with anything yet, but that doesn't mean you're off the hook. Not by a long measure. I'm going to take you along and get you settled in to one of the cells. Come along with me.'

The Painter creaked into an upright position and moved towards the door, which McMann now held open for him.

'Carry on along the corridor,' McMann announced, pointing the way and allowing The Painter to walk ahead of him. Around the corner, he discovered another desk manned by a young police officer in uniform. Detective McMann had overtaken The Painter and stopped in front of the desk. 'I've got a new resident for you.'

The desk officer looked up and smiled. He took out a small blue tray and announced to The Painter, 'Empty everything from your pockets, please, into this tray.'

The Painter took out his mobile phone, his car keys, his studio keys, and the wad of cash he had in his pocket. Both police officers stared at the amount.

'That's a good deal of money you've got there. Planning on leaving the country or something?' McMann asked.

'No,' The Painter replied.

The uniformed officer counted the money carefully, placed it in a small, clear plastic bag, and wrote the amount on it, before sealing it in full view of the detective. When he had gathered everything together, he placed the tray into a compartment in a designated filing cabinet. The officer then stood up and announced, 'This way.'

Both Detective McMann and The Painter followed the uniformed officer further down the corridor to the second metal door. A small room revealed itself where the uniformed officer pulled out a well-used ink tray and grabbed The Painter's left hand, forcing it onto the inkpad with a well-practiced move before placing it firmly on the left-hand side of a sheet of paper, which was already dated. He then repeated the move with The Painter's right hand. The Painter eyed the marks on the paper, before studying his stained fingers. The two policemen watched him carefully, the uniformed officer's face creased in confusion, before they moved on to another room at the end of the corridor. It had a peep-hole in it and a drop-down rectangular opening, for a food tray.

The uniformed officer took out a key and unlocked the door. 'In you go, then,' he told The Painter.

The Painter stepped inside the small, sparse cell. The walls were a dull, dirty cream colour, and the floor was made up of worn concrete. High on the far wall was a small window made of thick glass bricks, encased in bars on both sides. In the furthest reaches of the right corner was the ubiquitous CCTV camera, underneath which was a standalone metal toilet pan with half a roll of toilet paper next to it. In the opposite corner was a metal bed whose scratched frame matched the cream colour of the walls. Placed upon the low bed was a single blue crocheted blanket and a faded striped blue-and-white pillow. The ceiling was made of cracked, peeling plaster, painted the same colour as the walls. The only source of light was a bulkhead light-fitting with a metal guard surrounding it.

The door slammed shut behind The Painter and the key clunked around 360-degrees to lock him in.

CHAPTER 18

The Painter shuffled over to the bed and lay down on the blanket. The mattress underneath rustled and he put his hand on it to feel the plastic coating which enveloped it. The cell smelled musky with the remnants of disinfectant mixed with vomit. The air was chilly and there was no sign of any kind of radiator in the room for warmth.

He began to pull the crocheted blanket around his shoulders and body. It wasn't very large and he could hardly make both ends meet. He finally managed to pinch it shut with the fingers of his right hand. The wool was old and worn and smelled slightly of its former occupants, which he found mildly comforting.

The Painter stared hard at the empty brickwork opposite the bed. Its paint was cracked and chipped and there were a few indefinable words scrawled upon it. He twisted his legs around to face upwards in order to alleviate the pressure from his swollen testicle. Everything surrounding his skeleton seemed to pound, pierce and ache. Between the high and low density pain in his body, he was rendered unable to sleep.

He felt his way, with the fingers of his left hand, down under the mattress and onto the ragged, scraped coating of the bed's surface. He managed to peel a minute slither of paint away from its metal base and he held it up to his right eye. He could hardly make out the sharp spike of yellowing pigment. He brazenly pierced his bottom lip with it and a spot of blood formed on the skin's surface. He tasted its sterile content with the tip of his tongue and then viciously spat out at the wall opposite. The spit arced in the air then fell limply to the floor. There was no trace of blood in the spittle as it sat disconsolately on the cracked concrete.

The Painter began to shiver blindly at the cool, invisible draft which surrounded him. There was no appeasement to his condition: the cold, the pain, the light. He turned gingerly towards the window high above to view the sullen orange light which faded in through the thick glass and the metal bars.

The camera set up in the opposite corner burned its unblinking and unfeeling eye down relentlessly upon him. He tried staring back at it with the same unflinching stoicism, but his right eye blinked involuntarily within a few minutes and dry tears began to swell in their ducts.

The Painter reopened his cracked, bleary vision, the camera remained entirely unmoved by his predicament. It beamed down into his iris and remorselessly sucked up his every gesture and movement.

He glanced along the pattern of bricks on the opposite wall. Their relentless symmetry washed along the whole expanse, from corner to door. The Painter moved his left hand in space to feel across the wall's undulating geometric patterns.

On the ceiling there were cracks that tore their way crookedly to all four corners of the cell. The Painter lay on his back and stretched his left hand fully skywards then scratched some arabesques in the air to replicate the broken façade of the architectural confines of the box he now found himself within. The walls became a sculpted manacle, which squeezed the breath out of his lungs and bored his presence into his skull.

He tried pulling the blanket tighter around his shoulders. Pieces of it began to cautiously tear. He bit down into its straggly fibres and tasted the ennui and horror of all its previous inhabitants. The taste was a festering mass of lacklustre wool strands sated with alcohol, vomit, defecation, and weeping flesh.

The Painter cast the blue crocheted blanket onto the floor and pressed his head tightly into the rugged cotton of the striped pillow. It smelled of rancour and the rancid foulness of halitosis-ridden incontinence. The longer The

Painter sniffed at it, the more intoxicating it became. All the torments of hell were contained within its fibres, patiently awaiting their release from one inmate to another. His body responded to the infernal thoughts. His arteries widened and his heart pumped blood laboriously around his entire body. He gripped hold of the bed harshly as he began to weep. The tears stained the inside of his damaged left eye as they flowed from his right onto the deeply scarred and soiled pillow. They fell through the lining, down into the cheap polyester filling, to join their stagnant brethren.

Unconsoled, The Painter flung himself off the plastic mattress of the bed and onto the hard base of the concrete floor. He pressed down on his hands, pulled himself off his creaking knees, and staggered awkwardly towards the toilet pan. His bladder ached and demanded release, superseding all his other ailments.

Standing over the metal bowl, he unzipped himself. His penis pulsed as the urine poured out. It splashed against the sides of the pan and sprayed over the edges, hitting his shoes. When the final drips were scattered, he placed his penis back in his shorts and fastened his trousers. There was a round metal button in the wall and The Painter pushed it hard to release a rush of cleansing water into the toilet bowl.

The Painter returned laconically to the narrow metal cot. The blanket remained cast out on the floor as he lay down once more and shivered heavily. The cream walls appeared colder and closer than before. They seemed to illuminate every crack and imperfection in the masonry. He placed his hands above his head and began to scratch at the brickwork behind the bed. He listened attentively to the pathetic scraping of his hands clambering gracelessly against the hardened surface of the wall.

He then brought his hands to his face. Their nails were battered and broken, red, rough and calloused. The wound on his left palm was red; several attempts to scab over had been abandoned by his immune system and instead it wept from its inflamed centre, which beat out a pulse in time with his heart. The ends of his fingers emanated pain from every fibre and every nerve-ending in their system. He blew out a warm breath onto them in an attempt to revive them, or at least bring a little respite from the aggravating sting of their ripped ends.

The peep-hole in the door swivelled open noisily and an eye pressed itself up against the metal casing. It sought out The Painter lying in the corner on the bed. It remained for a moment unblinking, in unison with the camera above. The Painter remained stricken on the mattress, flickering his eye from camera to peep-hole and back again. Just as suddenly, the hole covered itself again and The Painter was alone in the cell with only the closed-circuit television camera for omniscient company.

In a corner of the room was a minuscule black object, which The Painter's truncated eyesight could just make out. He stared at it for a few moments, trying to discern its true outline. It looked like some kind of discarded piece of intransient waste. Intrigued, he dragged himself from his plastic-encased coffin and crawled on all fours towards the black dot.

When he arrived at the spot of the discarded object, The Painter discovered a creature of some sort: small and black, with legs. He picked it up in the pincer-like grip of his fingers and placed it on the open wound of his left palm. The creature showed no signs of consciousness and appeared to be perfectly dead. It was simply a black dot nestled within the confines of the red, raw, tissue of his flesh.

He placed it in his mouth, between his upper and lower front teeth, and bit down violently on the fragile corpse. He had the sensation of a vague crunch as the insipid creature was crushed. He rolled its broken body around his palate briefly before swallowing hard and squeezing its rough carapace down to the awaiting gastric acid in his stomach, to be dissolved into a putrid nothing.

Having completed this act, The Painter scoured the cell for further carrion. He moved in a crouched manner along the edge of the space, but there was little of any note to be found. A small piece of torn paper had retreated into another corner of the room. He picked it up and curiously examined it. The only thing he could make out was the letter 'X'. That was all that remained of whatever information that document had once contained.

The Painter returned to the bed and crouched down until his ear was virtually sitting on the concrete flooring and he could see quite clearly underneath the metal cot. The space was completely devoid of any detritus at all. He pulled himself painfully back up, took the small corner of paper he had found, and placed it in his pocket, before lying down once more on the bed.

The peep-hole in the door slid back and an eye was pressed up against it, as before. The Painter stared over at the blue iris, visualising the retina and the pupil, which stared back at him. The wide, devouring eye was framed within the door as though part of a giant, metal android machine. The only evidence of life was several blinks and the swivel to glance around the entire cell, before disappearing and being replaced by its steel eyelid again.

He turned his back on the door and faced the brick wall. It offered no oppositional view to the brick wall facing the other way. It could offer no solace. Its bricks held no warmth or comfort. The Painter lay shivering uncontrollably as he tried desperately to soothe himself into sleep. The light shining off the painted surface of the brick continued to blind his one working eye. The pain throughout his body was as relentless as before.

The Painter felt the seam of mortar breathe towards his

face. A cool breeze wafted uneasily over him and within it he heard a whispered cry, 'You are held prisoner by your own desires. You must transcend the self.' He moved his right hand out to touch the bricks, but he could feel no crack or fissure among them. There was no entrance or exit from the concrete-padded tomb imprisoning him.

He dug his nails into the wall and began to scratch hard at it until his blood began to carry along the seams of the cream bricks. He watched distractedly as they were repointed with the thin red streaks of his blood.

The Painter's stomach started to garble and he held onto it then pressed upon it tenderly. It suddenly began to contract a little in unison with his sphincter.

He rolled his way off the bed and scrambled towards the toilet. On the way, he unhooked his trousers and released them to the floor before pulling his shorts down to his knees. He plumped himself clumsily down on the low metal toilet pan and let his bowels eliminate their entire contents, which passed out quickly in broken spurts, punctuating the air with an extreme, sulphurous pungency. He whined slightly as sharp spats of pain echoed throughout his lower abdomen. After a few moments they were diluted into minor cramps, but he remained sitting listlessly on the toilet. When he finally felt able to raise himself up again, he pulled off a few reams of the rough toilet paper from a roll sitting at the side of the bowl, before pushing them up into his anus and clearing out the remnants of the waste still clinging to the sides.

He glanced down into the dilapidated, excreta-stained pan and paper, before swiftly pressing the button hard, to flush the toilet. He watched the water swish and swill out the pan, and return it to a level of relative cleanliness.

At the bottom of the toilet bowl there was a little piece of white debris sitting by itself. The Painter moved closer so as to view it more clearly. He sat down on his knees and hunkered over the metal pan. The spot of white seemed to gleam, redolent of some precious little gem. He reached his hand into the cold water and retrieved the discarded grit-like piece. Pinched between the ends of his fingers, he studied it closely. It was a tooth; it was his tooth.

The Painter examined the molar thoroughly before placing it in his mouth and fitting it within the very gap it had vacated earlier that afternoon. The tooth felt strangely alien. His gum had already moved on from the loss. He ground down on it, which pushed the tooth further into the wound in his mouth. The blood began to seep out of the sides of the hole which held the tooth. The Painter winced at the pain, which grew keener by the second. When it reached an excruciating pitch, he pushed the tooth free with his tongue and spat it back into the bottom of the toilet. A few spots of blood joined it and bobbed about in the small reservoir of water at the bottom of the pan. He left the toilet unflushed, allowing a red wisp of blood to break the surface, and returned to the bed.

As he lay down, The Painter stretched out and retrieved the blue crocheted blanket from the floor. He swathed the material around his head in an attempt to shut out the bright light emanating from the ceiling, but it was only partially successful. The wide weaves of the blanket allowed some light to filter through and reach the back of his pain-filled eyes. It produced a sparkling light-show in his right eye and a subdued glittering in his left. The colours swam around his head, creating kaleidoscopic reams of rainbow-inflected imagery. He laboured hard at his attempt to exclude all external stimuli and create a vacuum of blackness in which to nestle. But the light continued to radiate through in blocks, lines and streaks, which played through the outer rims of his eyelids.

The peep-hole slid open again, but The Painter remained fixated on his attempt to sleep. A key slotted noisily into its berth and then came the clanging of the lock and the door opening wide. A voice came at him from inside the cell. It sounded like a distant, faint echo which had come to torment him.

'Okay then, up you get, it's time to go.'

CHAPTER 19

The Painter showed no response until a hand shook his right shoulder and a gruff, but not unsympathetic, voice spoke over him, 'Come on then, wake up.'

The Painter gently unshrouded his head and stared, blinking, up at the police officer who had previously locked him in the cell. He gently swung his legs out of the bed and propelled himself up with as much gusto as he could muster. The officer grimly led the way out. The Painter stopped at the door and glanced back at the cell: the cream-coloured brick walls, the concrete floor, the cracked plaster ceiling, the bright, mesh-covered bulkhead light, the plastic-coated mattress, the blue crocheted blanket, and the metal toilet pan. He then pressed his face hard up against the tough, cold steel of the door. Its coolness stung his face and it smelled old, defiant and impenetrable.

At the end of the corridor, sitting on the desk, was Detective McMann.

The Painter peeled his face away from the door and followed the uniformed officer from the cell to the desk on which the detective sat.

McMann smiled at The Painter. 'How did you like your humble lodgings, then?'

The Painter didn't reply.

'I'd get used to those claustrophobic walls if I was you, it may well be the only kind of view you have for a very long time.'

The duty officer took out the tray which held The Painter's possessions in it and handed them to him one by one. The Painter gathered them up and placed them carelessly in his suit pockets. When this task was complete, the officer pushed a sheet of paper and a black biro towards The Painter. 'Sign this.'

The Painter looked down at the slip of paper. He took

the black pen and placed an X where his signature was required. He added a thumbprint as his hands were still soiled from having his fingerprints taken. The duty officer looked at the detective and they both shrugged their shoulders. Nothing could surprise them.

Detective McMann then moved off the desk and started to walk down the corridor. He indicated with his index finger for The Painter to follow him.

The Painter dragged himself after the detective, past the interview room they had inhabited together briefly. He held out his arms and touched both walls at the same time. The cool of the plaster sent a pleasant sensation through his fingertips and he closed his good eye for a brief moment. He couldn't feel or sense where he was and could only hear his own and the detective's footsteps.

At the end of the corridor was the small reception office where Detective McMinn was looking idly through some papers. The desk officer was preparing papers to be signed by a very presentable woman in her early forties, dressed in a tailored black jacket and skirt which she wore below the knee. She had a pair of black leather shoes with kitten heels and knotted around her neck was a black woollen scarf. She had a stern but attractive, slightly worn face and mid-length dirty-blonde hair. In her right hand was a brown leather satchel with two straps and a lock. She leaned over a desk and signed the papers the duty officer proffered to her.

'Here he is then,' Detective McMann announced.

The woman looked up at The Painter and stared at both detectives with consternation.

'What happened to my client?' she asked.

'Don't go getting your Jimmy Choos in a twist, love. That's how we found him.' Detective McMinn answered.

'It's not our style,' Detective McMann countered the accusation of police brutality she had implied.

The duty officer collected the papers and scrutinised

them for a moment, before announcing, 'He's free to go.'

'But not for long,' McMinn replied. 'It's bed and breakfast the hard way for you, my boy.'

'We'll be in touch soon,' promised Detective McMann.

The woman showed little emotion. 'This way. I've got a car waiting,' she stated coolly.

The Painter followed her to the door, where the duty officer calmly buzzed them out. It was a cold, starry night. The Painter sucked in the crisp, fresh air and filled his nostrils and lungs up greedily. He breathed in and out extravagantly for a few seconds. 'It's stopped raining,' he said to no one in particular.

They walked past two patrol cars and out through the gates. Waiting by the pavement was a black saloon car with tinted windows. The woman opened the back door and indicated that The Painter should enter.

Inside the car a middle-aged man sat in the driver's seat, dressed in a plain grey suit. In the back of the vehicle was a young man in his late twenties, dressed in a black pinstriped suit with a pink shirt and purple tie. He was clean-shaven, with short, thick black wavy hair. He was smoothly handsome, with an amenable air.

The Painter sat next to him as the woman slipped herself into the car in an effortless, self-assured manner, pulling the door shut as she did so. She then turned to face The Painter head-on.

'I'm Suzanne Dujardin, the legal counsel representing your gallerist Francesca Spilotti,' she offered her hand for The Painter to shake. Her hand was slender and warm and her grip firm. The Painter wanted to hold on to her hand, to feel the suppleness of the skin, the tenderness of the knuckles, in striking contrast to his own injured hand, but Suzanne quickly withdrew it.

'This is my colleague, Stephan Borowitz, he'll be representing you in this case.' Ms Dujardin indicated the man seated beside The Painter.

It was then Mr Borowitz's turn to take The Painter's hand. Stephan's shake was also firm and friendly, but his palm was clammier than Suzanne's.

'Don't worry, everything will be fine. We'll fight them all the way,' Stephan reassured glibly.

'The police got in touch with Francesca. They were wanting to speak to one of her employees, Emily. She wasn't available so Francesca asked them what it was regarding. They wouldn't tell her, but quizzed her instead and your name came up,' Suzanne explained. 'Then they disclosed that they were holding you at this station and so she got in touch with me to facilitate your release.' She paused and looked him over. 'I suggest that you get some rest and get cleaned up, then come into our practice on Thursday and Stephan will start to go over the case with you. If you can think of anything between now and then that can help us, write it down,' she finished.

'But don't show the police anything,' Stephan smiled.

'Never, ever talk to them again without Stephan being present, okay?' Suzanne said in a slightly stern manner.

'Here's my card. You can reach me day and night,' Stephan Borowitz slipped The Painter a white business card embossed with black lettering.

'Now, where can we take you?' Suzanne asked.

'To Urs,' The Painter replied without consideration.

'Where does he live?' Suzanne inquired.

The Painter took the mobile phone from his pocket and searched for his address. He showed the phone to Suzanne, who took it from him and passed it to the driver. He stared at it for a moment before nodding and then sending it back. The car began to move slowly off into the city's nightscape.

'Are you sure you wouldn't rather see a doctor?' Stephan asked with some consternation with regard to The Painter's physical condition.

'I'm okay,' The Painter answered.

'It wasn't anything to do with the police?' Stephan continued, gesturing with his hand to the many injuries The Painter was exhibiting.

'They claimed they had nothing to do with it,' Suzanne countered and raised an eyebrow to Stephan.

Stephan smiled, took out his mobile phone and pressed a few buttons on it, before taking a couple of photographs of The Painter.

'Still, it doesn't hurt to be thorough about these things. Maybe they did do it and maybe they didn't do it and maybe they'll never be able to prove it either way. Did they take a photograph of you when they first picked you up?'

'No.'

'Did they offer you medical attention?' Suzanne asked.

'No.'

'Well, well, this case is going along nicely, isn't it?' Stephan exclaimed.

The car fell silent as all three passengers and the driver watched the quiet city streets as the car cruised along. It was late and all the shops and businesses had closed. There were some bar lights still burning and a few denizens huddled cautiously around a few late-night food stands and a taxi-cab office. Occasional groups of people blurred their way into view. Two couples were walking and laughing drunkenly together. A few lone males were marching homewards, heads down, fists gripping keys in their pockets in case of sudden attack. A nonchalant drunk was urinating extravagantly on a tree. A grey-and-white cat darted across the road and disappeared furtively into a dark alleyway. There was a single female cautiously picking her way along a deserted street, the shop grilles all pulled down, her eyes searching warily around her. Other cars were speeding along the roads; there were some lorries and vans, and the inevitable scream of sirens. Two police cars sped past in pursuit of a pimped-up hatchback. An ambulance's lights could be spotted across the river, briefly mirroring The Painter's own journey, before turning off and charging into the hidden depths of the other bank. The Painter felt the smooth, tight leather of the seat beneath him. He felt with his finger along the seamless black material. It squeaked quietly beneath his finger and, when he moved slightly, it creaked briefly. The perfume of Suzanne and the aftershave of Stephan mingled in the air to create a sweet and citrus aroma within the sanitised interior of the car. He closed his eyes and gripped the underside of the seat to stop himself from falling headfirst into the warm lap of Suzanne. He turned his head towards Stephan instead and laid it against the back of the seat. There was a commotion going on outside somewhere in the street, but he couldn't open his eyes, they simply refused to budge.

He didn't hear the car stop; all he felt was the gentle rustling of Suzanne's hand on his shoulder. The Painter moved his head sluggishly and sucked in a line of drool which was running down the side of his mouth and onto the expensive leather seating.

When he opened his eyes, he recognised the black metal railings which announced his arrival at Urs' place.

'Do you feel okay?' Suzanne asked with professional concern.

'Yes,' The Painter replied, his entire body writhing in pain as he peeled his head from the seat and felt a ripple of queasiness move from the soles of his feet to his head. For a moment, he thought he might vomit on the floor of the car. His head desperately desired the release, but his stomach had no contents to respond in kind.

His one good eye gazed upon Suzanne and then Stephan with a disordered bleariness. He could barely form any response at all. A terror ran through him that he might disintegrate at any moment into a wash of biological tissue and matter which would slush through the doors of the car and drain out through the black metal railings into the cold, mutinous waters of the river.

'Are you sure you wouldn't rather we took you to get some medical attention instead?' Stephan asked kindly.

'I'm okay,' The Painter answered semi-coherently.

'Well then, get a good rest and we'll talk again,' Stephan checked his watch, 'tomorrow.'

Suzanne had opened the door and was standing in the street. The Painter crawled along the back seat of the car and clambered his way out.

Ms Dujardin assessed him once more and looked towards the building in front of them. 'Is this the correct place?'

'Yes,' he answered.

'In that case we'll bid you goodnight,' she offered The Painter her hand again.

He took it limply and she shook his hand rigorously.

'Don't worry, it's all in order, Stephan's a top man. He'll get you off,' Suzanne smiled briefly before slipping fluidly back into the car.

CHAPTER 20

The Painter stood and watched as the car rolled away, its red lights glowing distantly smaller as it drove further down the street, before disappearing altogether into the darkness beyond.

The chill of the night air made The Painter shiver convulsively. Out on the river, a boat chugged through the water with only a light by the bow showing it the way.

He turned to the warehouse building, its brickwork as dark and ominous as the river beyond. He sought out the intercom by the door and pushed in the button. He waited a moment but there was no response. He pushed the button again. 'Hello,' a voice said.

'I'm here to see Urs, about Hans,' The Painter explained.

The door clicked open and The Painter fell inside. He stumbled onto the floor in a crouched position with his left knee on the wooden flooring. He stared at the red sculpture positioned as it had been before, but lit differently to cast its shadow out from its core. The Painter looked up to view a set of lights dangling from the ceiling, beyond which was the darkened sky rising up above the city.

The Painter raised himself from the floor and pushed towards the metal staircase, which now seemed dark and brooding in the night light. He pulled himself by use of both hands up to the top of the stairs. The metal felt cold and alienating against his battered fingers. The living area seemed both stark and gloomy. There were two standalone metal lamps firing direct light from two corners of the large, floating space. Another wooden anchored lamp gave off a duller light from a third corner. Urs was reclining immodestly on the black leather sofa in a black silk dressing gown with an image of a red Chinese dragon snaking down the front left-hand side. He motioned for The Painter to be seated.

The Painter went to sit on the Eames chair but then thought better of it and sat in the padded leather chair instead.

'You have news of our mutual friend?' Urs smiled widely.

'He's dead,' The Painter answered wearily.

'Dead?' Urs sat up. 'What the fuck happened to him?'

'Murdered.'

'By whom?'

'Me, according to the police.'

Urs relaxed again. 'Well, well, my friend, frankly I wouldn't have thought you had it in you.'

'I don't,' The Painter stated unconvincingly.

'Of course not,' Urs winked at him.

A young man appeared by the doorway, dressed only in tight denim shorts. He was tall, handsome and tanned, with short black hair. He stared at The Painter without emotion. Urs turned his head on the sofa towards the doorway where the young man stood. He gazed at him momentarily before turning back to address The Painter. 'This is Luis,' Urs stated triumphantly.

'Luis,' The Painter repeated.

'You haven't met Luis, have you?'

'I met Rudi,' The Painter stated, confused.

Urs scowled at him violently.

'Rudi is not on the scene anymore. Luis is Brazilian. He only got off the plane a few weeks ago. He's very talented. Great voice. Does all these smooth jazz numbers. He's going to be a star. Isn't that right?' Urs said, turning again towards Luis, who was still standing pensively in the doorway.

'Why don't you fix me a whisky,' Urs said. 'And make one for my friend here, too. No water, just ice.'

Luis disappeared and Urs kept gazing at the doorway before turning back to focus his attention on The Painter.

'So, my friend, Hans is dead, murdered. That won't

work out well for those German photographers,' Urs grinned malevolently.

'I don't know,' The Painter replied.

Urs studied him for a moment then uncrossed and crossed his legs again. He was naked beneath the silk robe.

'What the fuck happened to you? You look like shit. In fact, you look worse every time I see you. Is it a woman? Have you got some married piece of ass squirrelled away somewhere whose husband keeps on catching you on the job and giving you a beating? But you can't stay away. You're a pussy-hound, right? All you artists are. You can't get enough of it. You can smell it now, wanting you, calling you, but you're going to get another beating for sticking your tongue up that snatch,' Urs started roaring with laughter as Luis walked through with two crystal tumblers filled with ice drenched in an amber liquid. He placed the two drinks on the glass coffee table in front of both men.

Urs viewed the glasses with suspicion as Luis left the room without saying a word. 'You'd think being a barman, he could fix a drink properly. Still, his talents lie elsewhere. He's got a good voice and he knows how to use it. He's from Rio, you know, and he's still got that taste of the sea about him. He's got really salty balls when you teabag them. It's like a taste of the tropics. Different to Rudi; not better as such, Rudi had his talents too, but different. You understand what I mean, my friend. Of course you prefer the pleasures of women,' Urs nodded to himself as though The Painter had responded. 'Sure, I understand, but it's causing you grief. Look at your face,' Urs gestured towards him before lifting his glass and taking a slug. 'Go ahead, take a sip. It's not poisoned and I'm not going to charge you for it.'

The Painter picked up the heavy weighted glass, its diagonal grooves nestling into his fingers. He smelled the raw texture of the liquid as it sizzled through his nostrils.

He then raised the glass fully to his lips and sipped at it. The taste was peaty and sweet, more smooth than abrasive as it passed down his throat.

'It's good my friend, no? This one's from up in Sutherland, at the top of Scotland. It's got a nice mellow palate, perfect for the melancholy of the night.' Urs raised his glass and took a swig from it.

The Painter's one good eye felt heavy and his head felt groggy from the scent and taste of the whisky. He laid the glass tumbler back down on the table with a leaden hand. It hit it, glass on glass, with a thump. It was enough to pull Urs' drink away from his lips as he studied The Painter's lumpen movements with some concern.

'You need to get some rest, my friend. You are not a healthy specimen of humankind. I realise this thing with Hans has probably upset you. I know he was a great collector of your work, but never mind, you'll find plenty of other willing clients. Without wanting to be unkind or to speak ill of the dead, fuck him,' Urs raised his glass to himself. 'In the end, it's the German photographers who will miss out on his patronage, not you, you've already had it.'

'The Germans?'

'You know, isn't it funny? The old cliché was that the only country that won the second world war was America, but it's not true. Look at the world today and what do you see? America won the war, sure, but who would have thought the other two great winners would have been Germany and Japan? Germany dominates Europe and Japan has continuously dominated Asia, or at least the Pacific rim. The two fucking countries which lost the war, actually, in the end, won,' Urs spread out on the sofa, warming to his subject. 'You know it's like the post-colonial landscape. Who are the countries emerging as world leaders, new alpha countries such as India, South Africa, Nigeria, Brazil, China. These are the future. These are the countries we're going to be working for. Sometime in the future they'll be exploiting our labour, we'll be their fucking servants,' Urs let out a raucous laugh. 'And so, my friend, the world keeps turning. Imagine the Arabs hadn't discovered oil? They'd be at peace. Nobody would have troubled them. It's only when you are of use that you are in danger. Don't forget that, my friend,' Urs drained his drink, before swishing the ice around to loosen enough fluid to take another gulp.

The Painter said nothing and he contemplated taking another sip of his drink. He thought better of it. The air in the room felt stale and pungent, the lighting was throwing off a depressed ring, and the designer furniture that his host was so proud of felt somehow bleak and dingy. He gripped hold of the side of his chair and hauled himself upright, moving as gracefully as he could manage to the doorway. Luis was nowhere to be seen. The Painter turned and looked back at Urs, who seemed to be sneering to himself somewhere in the middle distance.

The Painter gravitated to the stairway and bundled himself down towards the door. On the way down he engaged with a large, square painting on the wall, which he hadn't noticed before. It was covered in reds and oranges, some rich burnt umber, with a hint of yellow washing around in an intense undercoat. The painting was thick with master strokes of oil, rampaging across the canvas: exposing a deep vortex of colour, form and texture. The picture appeared to be aflame with echoes of life as seen under a microscope, or the universe viewed through a telescope. It was an apocalyptic vision of insanity and destruction, deftly and beautifully confined within the dimensions of the wooden stretcher which provided the only frame.

The Painter's right eye refused to focus on any consistent part of the pictorial plane. He blinked a few times and turned away from it before crashing down the last few stairs and landing on the hard flooring on his hands and knees. He spat bitterly onto the polished varnish, tears of rage running down his cheeks as he punched the floor as hard as he could. The pain forced his teeth down on his tongue and a bloody drool released itself from his mouth in one long, viscous droplet. He began to crawl towards the door on his hands and knees, hyperventilating. The handle to the door seemed impossibly out of reach as he looked up from his rigid position on his creaking knees and elbows. He laid his head down on the smooth, warm flooring and rolled his forehead back and forth across it. His eye wept a little fluid across the wooden boards, smearing across the tight expanse of skin at the front of his head.

Pushing against his knuckles, The Painter propped himself up against the door with his right shoulder. He pushed himself further upwards with the ends of his toes pressed down heavily on the ground. Slumping fully against the door, he pulled hard on the handle, before extricating himself from Urs' abode and finding himself once more outside in the chill of the night-time air.

It was a relief. The city was in repose. There was a distant chugging of engines somewhere out on the river, but no boats passed by. The black water lapped against the sides of the bank. The Painter stared desolately at the railings: a steel grille between him and that cold, detritus-ridden river.

The water appeared to swirl into a vague whirlpool out in the blackness of its flow. Words breathed over the surface to him, 'You are alone: we are all alone.' He walked over and gripped hold of the steel railings, cold and unyielding against his skin.

He wanted to gain entry to the river and plunge his delirious face into its purifying effluence. He wanted to sink down into the freezing dark cauldron to cleanse his flesh of all pain and subjugation. The icy waters would open themselves up and admit him before shrouding his corporeal state and dragging it down to the blackest depths, where it would squeeze all breath from his lungs and fill them with the sewer-drenched secretions of the surrounding city instead, abasing him forever in the discarded remnants of the mechanisms of its existence.

The Painter turned away and began his slow walk along the road leading up from the riverside. He stumbled along a pavement lit lovingly by strung-out lamp-posts. They left their triangulated expanse of orange light against the wall and the damp paving slabs, catching the hem of the failing light of the next lamp along. A chiaroscuro shroud creeping its way along the entire concrete carapace of the street.

He stopped in the full glare of one of the streetlights, unbuttoned his flies and pulled out his penis with his right hand, and urinated over the pavement. He held himself up against the straggly concrete pointing of the stone wall using his left hand, and pissed all over his shoes and the bottoms of his trousers. The splashes of urine against his ankles felt momentarily warm and comforting before cooling in the crisp night air. The pungent aroma hit his nose on a waft of steam.

The Painter traversed the street by staggering into illuminated spots before plunging into shadow then back into the brightly-lit spots again, all along the length of the road, which finally aligned with the junction to a major arterial route leading further towards the heart of the urban metropolis.

Up on the main road, The Painter grasped hold of an extravagantly-worked black metal streetlamp and gripped around the entirety of its embossed and elegant trunk. He panted lifelessly as he surveyed both quadrants in his path. His feet and head both craved the most efficient means of returning home and a wilful collapsing on his bed.

The night streets were strafed with cars and vans and

trucks, moving shiftily about the streets, searching out their quarry. A taxi crept along, its vacant light burning bright in the expansive road. The Painter threw his arm out desperately and the car slowed to review the prospective passenger before speeding away on its journey further into the dark of the night. The Painter kept his place, gripping his arm around the lamp-post and searching for the next cab to come along.

The drivers paid him little attention, each one caught in their own journey. Eyes and arms steered straight ahead, seeking out relief in the refuge of the lone city streets.

The Painter shivered as a cold breeze began to penetrate down to his skin. The night air was endless, as though the warmth of the dawn would never appear. He had no idea where he was, or how difficult it would be to make it back home. His hands felt around the cold enamelled metal of the street-light, which was propping him up vertically against the dementia of his fatigue.

An ambulance screamed by, its lights whizzing and its siren howling. The sudden jolt of this frenzied activity resurrected The Painter briefly and he flapped his arms about at any moving vehicle. A passing taxi-cab zoomed to a stop beside him. Its movement was so surreptitious that The Painter continued at first to watch the other traffic out in the road. He suddenly became aware of the dark roof of the car parked next to him, its vacant light reflected in his right eye.

The Painter fumbled around the back door of the car and searched out the handle. He gripped hold of something and pulled it outwards and the door swung open. The warm interior smelled of second-hand beer and contraband cigarettes. He felt his way inside, across the padded leather seating, until he found a niche by the door, which he slammed behind him with as much strength as he could muster.

'Where to?' the driver asked laconically through the

gaze of his mirror.

'The meat-market,' was all The Painter could manage before slumping his head against the window of the cab.

'Rough night, huh? You and a few others,' the driver spoke mostly to himself.

He pulled out into the oncoming traffic with a resigned aggression required to traverse the streets, weaving and dodging his way through one shortcut to another. He took main roads and long streets before darting through a couple of narrow one-way alleys. The streets were quieter than earlier in the night. Some delivery vans were doing their rounds, and there were refuse trucks parked up while men plucked black bags from carefully-constructed bales and pyramids. Lights blazed in the streets outside, but nothing much seemed to move.

The warmth in the back of the car exacerbated The Painter's fatigue, but it was tempered by the cry of the multiple sites of pain. It had welded his flesh to his nerve-endings and made it impossible for him to hone in on any particular part of his anatomy: he ached from head to toe and navel to sternum. His hands, his arms, his head and his face, his genitals, his knees, his mouth and his teeth, his ankles and his feet, all pounded, pulsed, quivered and stung. He was rendered incapable of experiencing any form of comfort. Pain had become the normal state of his being.

There was no further attempt at sleep. The pain felt as though it would never subside, as though it were there for all eternity. It was the only possible future he could contemplate. Gripping his fingers in his palms, he gave the illusion he could incapacitate the pain by rage and anger and helpless fatigue. The broken and battered nails tried piercing the already-opened flesh. It just added further to the strain and the indomitability of his nerve-endings. Pain was the absolute summation of his entire state of being: an infinite one, without reverse, appeal or salvation.

The taxicab slowed to a stop outside the meat-market. White vans, cardboard boxes, crates and trolleys littered the pavement outside. There was a flurry of activity, with men and women clothed in white coats, white trousers, white boots and white hats ferrying carcasses of varying sizes, weights and species into the covered warren of competing butchers.

The taxi driver grimaced as he observed all the skinned, gutted and headless animals slung over coarse shoulders with an indifferent bravado. 'Put you off your tea, wouldn't it?' he said.

The Painter fished into his pocket for a few notes and handed them over. The taxi driver tried to pass two back, but his passenger had already opened the door of the car and was alighting onto the pavement with as much dexterity as his exhaustion would allow. The driver shouted back some remark of gratitude, but The Painter was already closing the door.

He could hardly recognise the building across the road as his studio and home.

The night sky was reflected plainly against its windows. A couple of lights burned around the building at various points. It felt both welcoming and alienating, in equal measure.

He crossed the road and keenly managed to swerve out of the way of an approaching van. The stench from the market was suffocating his stomach and a wash of nausea lurched up towards his mouth, only to retreat half-way due to insufficient bile. As he reached the pavement on the studio side of the road, The Painter suddenly became aware of the pick-up truck with orange flashing lights hooking up the undercarriage of the battered Porsche. The driver pressed a button and the front end of the sports car lifted into position. The man then entered the cab of the towing vehicle and drove off with great purpose, proudly hitching his catch of the day.

The Painter stood still on the pavement and observed the movement indifferently, then glanced across the road at one of the meat-market workers, kitted out in red-smeared white, smoking a cigarette and smirking at the extrication of some tosser's luxury car.

The pungency of the odour drifting across the street on the prevailing breeze brought a desperate sense of decay. The flesh becoming pulp, the marbled skin becoming a parched translucence, the pinks and reds becoming purples and blacks. The Painter limped towards the steps leading to the entrance of his building and scrambled through his pockets for his keys. On the first attempt, he was unsuccessful. He pushed his left shoulder against the wooden doorway and, through a sheer act of will, attempted to gain entry. He finally relented and tried another key, at which point the door opened wide and he scattered himself onto the floor inside. He skidded vertically for a moment before lying horizontal on his back. As he looked heavenwards, he realised he hadn't noticed the ornate design on the ceiling before. There was intricate plasterwork producing grand baroque arabesques where no one would see it.

The Painter's head nestled against the hardness of the floor, inert and unable to lift itself upwards. He fumbled around with his hands and pressed them down to propel himself forward. His feet skated around the polished floor and with some difficulty he somehow managed to scramble himself upright again. He slumped his way towards the staircase and gripped hold of the varnished wooden banister with both hands. He then began to tug his way up the stairs to the first floor, swapping left hand with right all the way to the top.

He opened the door leading into the corridor outside his studio. The air in the enclosed space felt warm after the chill of the streets. The emergency lighting cast a gloomy reflection on the floor and walls, which was enhanced by the pin-sharp silence surrounding the building.

The Painter listened to his footsteps as he dragged himself past the studio door to avoid its dilapidation and on to the alternative entrance opposite the bathroom.

At the door, he clasped hold of the keys in his pocket and pulled them out. He tried the first key which came to hand but it wouldn't fit in the lock, no matter how hard he tried to force it. He made an attempt with another key to no avail, before he was successful with the third. This time he opened the door stealthily, to avoid falling inwards.

The flat felt warm and humid. It was dark in the passageway from the living space to the bathroom but there was a sticky, clammy feel to the air, with a vague trace of rotting decay matching the scents from the street below. The Painter stumbled his way into the bedroom area. Someone was lying naked on his bed, their skin caught in the half-glow of the streetlight outside. His hand fumbled around the wall until it came across a light-switch.

In the sharp overhead light of the room, The Painter recognised the still and silent figure on the bed as that of Emily. The deep red hair, the red lipstick and red nail polish stood in stark contrast to the dark, gaping wound that appeared to circumnavigate her entire neck. Her throat had been cut so deeply that it seemed as though her head would hang off her body if she was pulled into an upright position.

The Painter crept over to her naked form, her breasts and navel still wet with her blood. The parquet flooring was dowsed in a scarlet pool, which seemed to have run everywhere. Bundled by the bed was a red coat, a white shirt, black trousers, black high-heeled shoes, a black-and-pink bra, and a pair of pink-and-black knickers.

He stood next to the bed and peered down at Emily's green eyes, glassy and dull, staring straight up to the ceiling. Her lips were slightly parted, as though she were about to let out a sigh. Her entire body was pale and devoid of any sign of life. Her posture was stiff and forced. The wound across her throat was horrific in the extreme. The skin had parted ways to allow the blood to quickly flow out. The Painter slumped down on the bed beneath Emily's feet. He pressed his head into his hands and started to dig his nails into his face as hard as he could, in an attempt to tear at the skin.

As he looked at the wall opposite, he saw the great circular spray of blood arcing across it. On the floor beside the pool of blood was a discarded, bone-handled, straight razor with a glistening smear of icy scarlet gore staining the steel blade.

He touched the pinkish-grey soles of Emily's feet, which were totally devoid of warmth. Emily was dead and her presence would never return. She was now just a lump of biological matter. A corpse lying eternally dormant.

The Painter laid his face against her feet and started to kiss the cold, wilting flesh.

He slipped himself off the bed and crawled towards the large, deep red stain on the floor. He tried to scoop as much blood as he could in the palm of his right hand. It congealed on his skin as his hand became damp with the viscous, metallic fluid. He brought the splash of blood up to his mouth and began licking at it as tears ran down his face. His left eye chose this moment to crack open slightly, but the awful sight was thankfully shrouded in a blurry numbness. The blood was noxious on his tongue and mouth and the stickiness felt oppressive against his face as he tried to pour it back into Emily's lifeless body. But she remained immovable on the bedsheets, her organs no longer functioning; her words silenced forever.

The Painter retched aggressively and a minor trickle of bile merged with the blood on the floor and on his chin. He turned to look at Emily's body again and his stomach convulsed violently in mourning.

He leapt towards the light-switch, skidding on the blood on the floor on the way. He smacked the switch with his wet palm and the room returned to a nocturnal ambience. Emily remained half-lit on the bed, the wound around her neck densely illuminated by the outside light now being aided by the rise of a pale glow beginning out in the east.

'Covering up your handiwork?'

The question came from the other side of the living space.

The Painter swung around to face a silhouette framed in the doorway to the studio. It was the outline of a tall, slender male, but The Painter couldn't make out his face. He moved towards the dark shape without switching on the light. The intruder turned on the lights in the studio instead. The Painter half-recognised the man standing before him, wearing a slim grey suit with a light blue shirt casually unbuttoned at the neck.

'I've seen you before,' The Painter said as he stared into the man's bloodshot, heavily shadowed eyes.

'I'm Stephen Cornell-Jones, your gallerist's husband, seeing as you seem to have lost your memory.' He pushed past The Painter to walk over to the bed. 'But don't think the police will buy that when they're charging you with murder,' he said, looking back at The Painter.

Cornell-Jones stretched out his hand as though to touch Emily's, but withdrew it curtly, before putting his left hand over his mouth and sobbing a little. He gestured with his right hand towards her. 'She was so young and beautiful and talented. Now look at her. Look at what you've done to her. Why did you do that to her?'

Stephen Cornell-Jones sat down at the end of the bed. Emily remained in the same position as before: eyes determinedly fixated on the ceiling. 'I was in love with her. I was so in love with her. I was going to leave Francesca for her. I was going to help her set up her own gallery. She was so brilliant. She made me happier than I've ever been. And now look at her. Dead.'

'Why are you here?' The Painter asked, ignoring the implication that he had murdered Emily. He remembered her in his bed. He was pretty sure he hadn't hurt her.

'Francesca came to look over your studio and flat when she found out you were arrested last night, to make sure there wasn't any incriminating evidence against you. When she got here, she said that she found Emily lying murdered on your bed. I came over to see for myself.' Cornell-Jones paused a moment before declaring, 'She knew, of course.'

'Knew what?' The Painter enquired.

'That I was having an affair with Emily. We've known about each other's indiscretions for years. She takes her lovers and I take mine. Of course, we cover it up, play the game. I would tell her I had to go away to Antwerp or Tel Aviv on business for the family jewellers', but she knew what was really going on. With Emily it was different, though. We had a secret apartment that we rented where we used to spend time with each other, away from the world and its prying eyes. With Emily it was different. With Emily it was love.'

'Love.' The word seemed unfamiliar to The Painter.

'Yes. Love. I loved her. I wanted to be with her only, but it was complicated. I wanted to give Francesca some time.'

'Time?' Queried The Painter.

'She's having some trouble with the gallery, because of the economy. She had to buy up your paintings to protect their value. They were being dumped on the market. But then you knew that. I assume it's why you killed Hans Zimmer.'

'Hans,' The Painter stood, confused. The house he had awoken in; had he fought Hans and ended up injured? 'My paintings,' he mumbled to himself.

'You owe her so much,' Cornell-Jones stated angrily, breaking into The Painter's train of thought.

'Who?'

'Francesca.' Cornell-Jones went to touch Emily again, but couldn't bring himself to do so. 'Why kill her?' He asked The Painter.

'I didn't,' The Painter replied.

Cornell-Jones swept aside his denial. 'Was it because she wouldn't sleep with you? I noticed you leaving with her after the exhibition. She was supposed to rendezvous with me later, while Francesca was taking care of some business with that awful little fag Urs von Madsen. She somehow managed to get him to purchase one of your paintings. You see what she's done for you.

'But Emily never showed up at the apartment and she hadn't been seen since. Now we know what happened to her. You got her back here and tried to get her to have sex with you. But she wouldn't. I knew her better than anyone. She would never have done that. Never have betrayed me. But you artists and your superegos. You can't accept no for an answer. You can't comprehend it. You have to have everything your own way. You don't know what loyalty is. You don't think that you're privy to the same rules and laws as the rest of us. The schmucks who do the real work while you piss about in your studio with your paint. She thought you were a joke. They all do. Even Francesca. But she's loyal. Right to the end.' Cornell-Jones took several deep breaths, composing himself.

'Francesca,' The Painter mouthed the word. Now he understood. He stared at his blood-soaked hands. He hadn't killed anyone in his life. He was sure of it. He wasn't capable of it. He and his paintings were nevertheless somehow still to blame for the carnage.

Emily was dead, lying slaughtered on the bed, her throat slit so she couldn't take Francesca's husband, or steal her artists away to her new gallery. Hans was half-buried in the ground, a wooden splinter from a stretcher in his throat, so that he couldn't dump The Painter's work and ruin Francesca. Dan Smithson was garrotted by piano wire and crucified to his floorboards, so that he couldn't ruin Francesca's reputation and send her to jail by revealing how she had bought back The Painter's work to boost its value.

'Francesca,' The Painter said out aloud again with more force. 'Francesca did it.'

This time Stephen Cornell-Jones heard him. 'What did you say?' he scorned.

'Francesca did it. She killed them all,' The Painter repeated.

Cornell-Jones had risen from the bed.

'What are you saying?' he shouted angrily.

The Painter looked directly at him. 'Francesca killed her,' he stated calmly.

'You fuck. You vicious little cunt,' Cornell-Jones spat at him, picking up the razor from the ground. 'You've ruined my fucking life,' Cornell-Jones screamed out as he slashed at The Painter with the razor. He caught him in the neck, splitting his Adams apple open with the blade. The Painter gripped at the deep gash on the front of his throat instinctively as the blood began to course out of the wound, joining the drying blood of the girl who had been his only help.

Cornell-Jones took another raging lunge at him, but this time The Painter held up his left hand. The razor sliced right down the length of his knuckles and the blood began to gush everywhere. In spite of himself, The Painter couldn't fail to appreciate the patterns which were spreading across the floor. Perhaps this could be his commission for The Siberian.

The Painter staggered through into the heart of the studio, pursued by Cornell-Jones, who screamed and lunged at The Painter for a final time but The Painter managed to grab Cornell-Jones' wrist as the razor came towards his face.

The two men grappled with the deadly weapon as The Painter bled steadily over Cornell-Jones and his own studio floor.

As they wrestled with each other, Cornell-Jones was finally able to throw off his enfeebled victim, who crashed against a pot of paintbrushes, scattering them randomly across the worktop.

The Painter desperately grasped hold of a thick brush and, turning as swiftly as he could, plunged it deep into the neck of Cornell-Jones, who immediately stumbled backwards with a look of absolute shock and supreme terror as he tried to extricate the piece of wood from his flesh. He managed only to snap the brush in two, leaving a sharpened piece of wood protruding from the left side of his neck. The blood was spraying out from all sides of the wound and covering the walls of the studio in red gore.

Cornell-Jones slipped on a spillage of yellow paint on the floor and staggered backwards before impaling himself on a canvas stretcher with the broken paintbrush.

He lay slumped against the woven cotton, pinned to it by the splinter of wood protruding from his neck, blood flowing out of his throat and covering the canvas's surface area. The Painter noted with some satisfaction that Cornell-Jones' eyes now held the same expression as Emily's and Dan Smithson's had: unblinking and staring into a distant future which they would never see.

The Painter, panting and bleeding, collapsed against a wall. He sat there, immobile, watching the blood flow freely from his wounds. The pain in his body was lessening as the blood ebbed away.

On the bed next door, Emily lay naked on the mattress with her throat cut. She was as dead as Hans Zimmer, Dan Smithson and Stephen Cornell-Jones. She was as dead as the only boy she had ever loved, who had lain naked in a mortuary on a slab of steel.

Soon, The Painter would belong with them. His eye could hardly focus on the room, which was flooding with the colour red.

He watched the sun climbing from its nocturnal slumber. Another day was dawning and it was casting its warm orange glow through the window and across the floor of the studio.

The Painter stretched his hand out to greet it, but he could feel nothing anymore.

There was the voice, 'I no longer feel connected. I am disappearing.'

The Painter searched around the studio, but couldn't locate the source.

The words were the last thing he heard.

THE END

If you have enjoyed this book, we would be very grateful
if you would take the time to review it on the Amazon
website. A positive review is invaluable and will be
greatly appreciated by the author.

Please also visit the Heddon Publishing website to find out
about our other titles: www.heddonpublishing.com

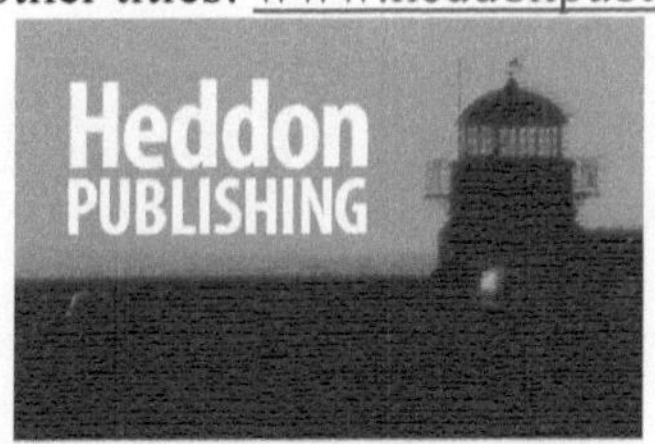

Heddon Publishing was established in 2012 and is a
publishing house with a difference. We work with
independent authors to get their work out into the real
world, by-passing the traditional slog through 'slush piles'.
Please contact us by email in the first instance to find out
more: enquiries@heddonpublishing.com

Like us on Facebook and receive all our news at:
www.facebook.com/heddonpublishing

Join our mailing list by emailing:
mailinglist@heddonpublishing.com

Follow us on Twitter: @PublishHeddon